The
Computer
Based Training Handbook

Assessment, Design, Development, Evaluation

The Computer Based Training Handbook

Assessment, Design, Development, Evaluation

William W. Lee & Robert A. Mamone
with contributions from Kenneth H. Roadman

Educational Technology Publications
Englewood Cliffs, New Jersey 07632

Library of Congress Cataloging-in-Publication Data

Lee, William W.
   The computer based training handbook : assessment, design,
development, evaluation / William W. Lee, Robert A. Mamone with
contributions from Kenneth H. Roadman.
      p. cm.
   Includes bibliographical references and index.
   ISBN 0-87778-286-5
   1. Electronic data processing--Study and teaching. 2. Computer
-aided instruction. I. Mamone, Robert A. II. Roadman, Kenneth H.
III. Title
QA76.27.L43 1995
004'.071--dc20   94-46482
                                                              CIP

Dedicated to:

Goldie, Philomena, and Dharmarajoo, whose love, guidance, friendship, and support have inspired and sustained us.

and

In Memory of:

Tim Kairis (1967-1990),
our friend, who had so much to give and was taken from us too soon.

Foreword

This book is designed to assist companies in the completion of their Computer Based Training (CBT) projects. It can be just as easily used by the novice as the experienced project development team. It can be used by teams that develop CBT for use internal to their company or by those who develop CBT for external customers. It can also be used as a text by the student of computer based instructional design.

Based in the traditional five-phase design and development process, we have provided a no-nonsense approach to CBT project completion. The text minimizes theory and provides step-by-step strategies that have resulted in successful projects time after time. Not that theory is unimportant! We have included the theory in a section of each chapter entitled Rationale so that you can explain to your internal or external customers and other designers why you are using certain strategies in a project.

The text begins each unit with an Introduction that explains what will be covered in the unit. Each chapter introduces the topic of the chapter, then explains "What to Do" and "How to Do It." The "what" lists those tasks that must be completed during each phase, and the "how" explains the ways to go about completing each task. The Application Tools section of each chapter provides examples of document outlines, worksheets, review forms, and checklists that will help complete each task.

This book does not cover project management in detail. Educational Technology Publications has two excellent books on Project Management: one written by Michael Greer and the other by Robert Bergman and Thomas Moore. These are both referenced in several places throughout this book and can be consulted by readers who wish to have the widest possible knowledge in this area. Educational Technology also publishes an excellent text on all facets of developing interactive multimedia instruction, by Richard Schwier and Earl Misanchuk, and a leading text on the fundamentals of instructional design, by Cynthia Leshin, Joellyn Pollock, and Charles M. Reigeluth. These books are referenced in the Bibliography.

Our hope is that our book will help CBT project teams avoid many of the obstacles that we have encountered in our collective 75 years in the field of CBT development. You should read through the entire book to understand the overall concept of CBT development that we outline. Then the book can be used as a handbook and reference during projects to make your job easier. We welcome your comments on the usefulness of this book in assisting you in your endeavors.

Table Of Contents

List Of Tables

NUMBER AND NAME OF TABLE   **Page**

List Of Figures

UNIT 1

Introduction

Tom, the program manager for our CBT project, hosts the kickoff meeting with the customer and the entire project team, where he reviews all of the requirements of the contract and lays out the entire project for everyone who is involved.

THE IMPORTANCE OF THIS BOOK TO YOU

Whether you have just gotten your first Computer Based Training (CBT) assignment from a customer[1] or you are just tired of reinventing the wheel every time you get a contract, this book should help. We remember how we felt when we got our first contract to develop a CBT course. The feeling was how a dog must feel when it chases a car and finally catches one! What does it do with it now? We wanted the project; we bid the project; we had all of the Instructional Design expertise from our training background and education.

---

[1]When we refer to customer throughout this book we mean both external or internal customers to your organization, as appropriate in each instance. That is, you may be working either as an internal CBT team, or as an outside consultant in the field of CBT design and development.

Don't Reinvent The Wheel

But what we discovered very quickly was that the theory we had learned and the little practical experience we had on projects in college and on developing non-CBT courseware needed to be adapted to the special requirements of Computer Based Training. Many aspects were similar but many additional requirements — or modifications to familiar practices — were needed to complete such a project.

During a project, with the normally "ambitious"[2] schedules, there is little time to document a process or procedures. We use the saying, "When you're up to your neck in alligators, it is difficult to remember that your initial purpose was to drain the swamp." If your company is like many of the companies we have worked for, they move right on to the next project when one is finished, and there is little or no time to write down the things that worked and those that didn't. Since a new team is usually assembled for each project, with different people and new hires assigned, each team member has his or her own ideas about ways and means to complete each task or step. This often results in a "loss" of prior process improvements.

How To Use This Book

This book is our effort to never have that confusion happen to us again. Hopefully, it will also help you avoid the "scrambling" that takes place throughout each project to solve unexpected events.

If you need an entire process for your first project, use this one as the basis and adapt the procedures as you go along. Or, you can use it in its entirety and then make changes for your next project. If you already have a process in place, this book can help you smooth out some rough spots that might exist by giving you another perspective and other ideas about ways to accomplish a particular task.

Many books on the Instructional Systems Design (ISD) Process — also known as the Instructional Design and Development (ID&D) Process — will tell you what to do to complete a CBT project. Some will also tell you why. This book is the first that actually tells you *how* to complete each task required for the successful completion of a project.

The ISD Process that we outline throughout this book has worked for us in many software environments (Macintosh, DOS, Windows, just to mention three). It is hardware and software independent. You will need to adapt some of your Course Design Specifications to the particular environment you are in. (For example, a DOS environment limits the number of characters you can use in file names to eight, but Macintosh permits file names of many more characters.)

The Chapter References found at the end of each unit cite only those that we directly used in a particular chapter. We have included a Bibliography that

---

[2]The word "ambitious" is used here as a euphemism for "crazy."

provides a list of works that will supply you with a more in-depth coverage and information, including material on topics relevant to but outside the immediate scope of this book.

UNIT CONTENT

This Unit will cover:

1. **CBT: The Solution to Information Overload**
2. **Four Levels of CBT**
3. **Compatibility of CBT with Adult Learning**
   Independence
   Learning Environment
   Learner Control
   Principles of Learning
4. **Cost-effectiveness of CBT**
   Benefits of CBT
   Up-front Cost
   Consortium Concept
5. **Configuration Control**
   Version Control During Development and Review

CHAPTER 1-1
CBT: THE SOLUTION TO INFORMATION OVERLOAD

THE INTERACTIVE AGE

No longer do we talk about the "information age." The newest term is the "interactive age." In the information age, the amount of information that was being created was increasing more rapidly than at any other time in history. There was no way that businesses or individuals could stay current on all trends, topics, or issues.

Computers were both the cause and the solution to the problem. Computers made the amount of information that could be generated and disseminated almost limitless. At the same time, computers made the amount of information that a person could receive just as boundless. Sorting through the information was at the same time a greater feat, but could also be accomplished more rapidly. Information databases were available through modem hookups or on a 4- inch CD ROM — both of which could come directly into your home or office.

Providing training also became easier with satellite hookups that could be downloaded from one central location to virtually anywhere in the world. Thousands of people could take the training at the same time, or the material could be stored and used later at a more convenient time. This became a very important capability for companies that had gone multinational, had diversified holdings, or had decentralized. The cost of travel, lodging, and lost productivity was making it prohibitive for companies to bring employees to one central location for training.

THE IMPACT ON BUSINESS

At the same time, with information advancing so rapidly, there was no such thing as standing still in business. If you weren't moving forward, you were moving backward. CBT was seen as a viable solution to keeping current. Even though the up-front investment in training was larger, for companies that fit the categories above and who delivered a massive amount of training, CBT was very cost-effective in the long run.

THE IMPACT ON INDIVIDUALS

Now that we are in the "interactive age," not only can we receive information in our homes and offices, we can send it. We can sit at home and order virtually any of the goods and services we desire through our TV screen and a remote switch. It is now possible to order a car: see a picture, check colors, negotiate a deal with the dealership, arrange the bank loan, and have the vehicle delivered to your front door, without ever leaving your home. Then why do we need cars if we don't have to leave the house? To take advantage of all of the leisure time that we have on our hands, of course. Leisure time for everyone, it seems, except the people who have to develop the software and the training that brings this convenience!

The long-dreamed of ability to work from our homes, send the information to the office and only go in once or twice a week, is a virtual reality. With the addition of video phone capabilities and conference calling, large office buildings may not be necessary at all. CBT will be an even more critical component as we move further into the interactive age.

CHAPTER 1-2
FOUR LEVELS OF CBT

INTRODUCTION

What do we mean by CBT? We broadly define CBT as any form of training that is delivered (1) primarily through the interactive medium of the computer, or (2) through the computer with supplemental materials, such as student manuals, job aids, etc. Computer Assisted Instruction (CAI) is instruction that uses the computer as a part of instruction, possibly supplemental, but not the main medium of delivery. Interactive Videodisc (IVD) training adds the dimension of motion video and audio to the graphics capability of CBT or CAI by adding a laser disc player. Digital Video Interactive (DVI), a proprietary product, is very much like IVD, but the storage capacity is digitized on a CD ROM and the hard drive within the computer, making it possible to store and retrieve much larger programs on a personal computer while requiring fewer peripherals.

LEVELS OF CBT

This book does not deal with hardware as such. Hardware systems are advancing at such a rapid pace that the information would be outdated before this book got to print. However, we do want to list the basic levels of CBT because each level adds a new dimension that affects the cost and complexity of development. We have synthesized our definitions from several sources (Floyd *et al.*, 1982, and The United States Air Force, Air Force contract definitions).

The key to successful CBT development is to give the internal or external customer and the end user the least expensive and least complicated delivery system possible, but still meet all of their needs and expectations.

Level 1

Level 1 CBT involves the use of some variation of a video viewing device and a monitor. All control comes from the video player. There is no external computer control of the presentation. The video is linear and interaction is limited to starting and stopping the presentation. The delivery systems at this level are much like videodisc, CD ROM, or video cassette players that play without interruption. Examples of Level 1 programs are commercial movies that are played on videodisc or audio CDs.

Level 2

Level 2 CBT involves either internal or external computer control of the video presentation. A videodisc player with search capabilities can access particular frames. There is limited interaction from the student (making basic choices from a menu), but, after that, the information is very linear — everyone gets the same presentation. Level 2 is comparable to an information kiosk in an airport or a shopping mall where you can make a selection and receive information on locations of shops or gates, tickets, flight arrivals, hours of operation, etc.

Level 3

Level 3 CBT involves the use of a computer, videodisc player or DVI configuration, video monitor, and peripherals. This level provides for a high level of interaction and control and is the first level where individualization of instruction occurs. Instructional events are student controlled, and low to middle levels of simulations occur.

Level 4

This level of CBT is the most sophisticated and includes full simulation capabilities. Information is highly individualized and complex with multiple levels to accommodate student needs, and it progresses to higher and higher levels of sophistication. Information is presented through audio, video, and text; represents real-life situations that could be experienced, which are presented in the way that they would actually be experienced. Learning is usually more inductive than didactic. An example is a full motion video aircraft simulator that provides students with opportunities to practice flight maneuvers while removing the dangers of actual flight. Virtual reality simulations are the highest form of this level, providing the full range of audio, visual, and tactile/kinesthetic experiences. An example of a simulation that each of us might be familiar with, although at a lower level, is a video arcade game which presents multiple levels as players become more skilled at the game. Level 4 can apply to mid-level simulations as long as:

(1) programming provides for multiple branching based on student input; and
(2) feedback responds to student input in a highly specific manner.

PROGRAMMING/AUTHORING TOOLS

There are many programming tools available, from coded languages to authoring systems. Authoring systems can be very complex, requiring a special computer platform. Or they can be simple and inexpensive and can run on any computer just by inserting a floppy disk and following simple installation instructions. The simpler authoring systems are not as powerful with respect to their capabilities (branching, video, graphics, etc.), but will still fill many needs. The key is to give the customer the right tool to do the job, and as inexpensively as possible.

There is a further discussion about authoring tools in Chapter 4-2, and a list of many common ones is found in Appendix B. We do not spend a lot of time on this subject because we are not making choices for you. You probably have a Management Information Systems (MIS) department in your company that makes those types of choices. You have enough to do just designing the CBT! You do have to know the capabilities of the system chosen, as those capabilities affect your design. On the other hand, if all system choices, in your situation, are in fact at your discretion, then we suggest reviewing Milheim's (1994) *Authoring-Systems Software for Computer-Based Training*. This text compares and contrasts leading systems in great detail.

CHAPTER 1-3
COMPATIBILITY OF CBT WITH ADULT LEARNING

INTRODUCTION

The conditions under which training is delivered to children is often not suitable for adults. Adults require more control over their learning environment and more freedom with respect to where, when, and under what circumstances training is delivered. Children need guidance and supervision to establish the skills that will make them independent thinkers and self-sufficient learners. Although many adults may not possess the elements of adult learning that are required, they still demand that they be treated as if they do. This makes the computer an ideal method of delivery of training, but, at the same time, those principles that govern learning must be much more purposefully embedded in the training.

ELEMENTS THAT CONTRIBUTE TO LEARNING

Learning Environment

Adults learn best in an environment that is non-threatening and where they can progress at their own rate. They need the individualization that promotes accelerated learning, which allows them to move at their own particular pace, and which concentrates on those aspects of the training that they need, at that time.

Adults have little patience sitting through training where everyone gets the same information at the same time and at the same pace. If they know the information, they become bored, and by the time they get to the parts they need to know, they have often tuned out the training completely.

Since many adults have had a less than positive experience as children in school, the traditional classroom with an instructor conjures up negative experiences and makes learning less effective. In addition, the adult mind wanders (as evidenced by the well-researched fact that both program spots and TV commercials last less than 30 seconds). In the traditional classroom, the students can be physically present yet may tune out the entire training course. This "tuning out" causes higher rates of failure, which results in less effectively trained individuals.

In dealing with attention span, the computer is infinitely patient. If the students' minds wander or they become distracted, it will wait for them to refocus on the task. With high rates of interactivity and branching capabilities embedded in the program, if information is missed, the student can review it or receive reinforcement by being asked a question on the topic.

Individualized Instruction

The individualized instruction that the computer can deliver also provides for students to concentrate more heavily on the information that they do not know or have difficulty grasping. As opposed to traditional classroom learning where students often get "one shot" to grasp the material, the computer allows them to return to information as many times as they require or desire. This concept of "over learning" creates a condition where higher rates of information are attained and retained.

Interactivity

No one learns well in an environment where they are passive learners, detached from the learning experience. It is nearly impossible for instructors to get everyone involved in every learning situation by virtue of the ratio of students to instructor. The computer, though, gets every student involved.

Systematic Instruction

For complex tasks, the computer can systematically break a task into its component parts, teach each step of the task, then put the entire task back together. The computer can demonstrate a more holistic approach to a concept, teaching the task globally. The computer can even teach students the same task both ways, depending upon their learning preference. It is more difficult to break down each task and to meet individual learners' needs with traditional teaching methodologies.

An added advantage to CBT is that all students receive the same basic course — no concepts missed or given different emphasis — except that branching allows for more or less depth of instruction depending on what the student needs. Sophisticated programming can make the judgments about the depth of instruction required, based on student input.

Multi-Sensory Approach

It is best to learn information through as many of the senses as possible. Using a multimedia approach, the computer delivers training both visually and auditorially through text, graphics, video, and sound. Even tactile experiences are possible in higher level simulations[3]. Each medium reinforces the other, and the same material can be grasped by students who learn through different modalities.

Feedback and Reinforcement

Students need immediate feedback, especially when they are beginning to learn a new concept. Traditional instruction does not allow for high rates of responses from a large number of students. Usually, the first time a question is answered correctly by a student, the instructor moves on. What about the students who had the incorrect answer in their minds? They find out their answer was wrong, but they may never know why. Computers permit all students to participate and find out if their answers are correct and incorrect based on their own individual responses.

---

[3]Imagine the feelings of turning upside down in a flight simulator where you experience the exact sensations that you would feel in an actual plane.

APPLICATION OF LEARNING PRINCIPLES TO CBT

David Lillie, and his associates, Wallace Hannum and Gary Stuck, in their 1989 book *Computers and Effective Instruction*, provide a very comprehensive list of principles of learning and their application to the design of CBT. We provide an adaptation for adult learning of the work of these authors here to reinforce the importance of their work.

Principle 1

Students learn more when lessons begin with a review of previous material.

Application to CBT

Known as an Advance Organizer, effective CBT lessons begin with a review of relevant information. This review should consist of the basic premise of the previous lesson with respect to how it relates to what students will learn in the current lesson.

Principle 2

Students learn more when lessons and activities are introduced and learning objectives are specified.

Application to CBT

Effective CBT lessons state the lesson objectives and explain the purpose of the lesson in order to orient students to the subsequent material and the concepts that will be presented.

Principle 3

Students learn more when verbal content is precise and is presented fluently.

Application to CBT

Lessons must present material in very clear, precise language and move logically (make transitions) from one segment to the next, avoiding unnecessary interruptions or digressions.

Principle 4

Students learn more when relevant examples and demonstrations are provided to illustrate concepts and skills.

Application to CBT

The computer not only has the capability of explaining a concept, it can then guide students through examples that reinforce the concept. This principle is known as guided practice. Students can interact with the examples, provide input, or judge the correctness or value of the example. The computer program provides guidance and/or follows a variety of tracks based on student choices.

Principle 5

Students learn more when they are able to handle tasks and questions with high rates of success.

Application to CBT

Design lessons that ensure success for students who learn at different rates through incorporation of branching, reviews, and summaries.

Principle 6

Students learn more when lessons and instructional activities are presented through concepts and language that are understandable and appropriate to the intended audience.

Application to CBT

Develop materials that are based on your students' abilities, derived from Audience Analysis. Materials must be written at the appropriate audience level so that reading (text) or verbal (audio) language does not interfere with the concepts to be learned.

Principle 7

Students learn more when lessons are presented at a brisk pace and when instruction slows to accommodate students' understanding, but avoids unnecessary slowdowns.

Application to CBT

Effective lessons are individually paced because they allow students to move through material as slowly or rapidly as they require to fully understand the material.

Principle 8

Students learn more when transitions between lessons are made efficiently and smoothly.

Application to CBT

Students need to be reminded (cued) when the shift is made from one topic to the next or from one activity to the next. This can easily be done in CBT through the use of graphics, text, or audio prompts (reminders).

Principle 9

Students learn more when clear and concise assignments and directions are provided.

Application to CBT

    Lessons must include summaries after each topic and at the end of a lesson or concept. Directions for activities and tests must be clearly spelled out for students.

Principle 10

Students learn more when clear, firm, and reasonable standards are maintained.

Application to CBT

    Lessons must require students to demonstrate their mastery of the material presented. The computer can set basic standards for all students and present material to that baseline while still allowing for individual learning rates and styles.

Principle 11

Students learn more when instructors circulate during classroom assignments to check all student performance.

Application to CBT

    The computer is the "instructor" for each individual student. It can effectively check each student's progress and provide praise or remediation, both of which are necessary to keep students on task and progressing through the training.

Principle 12

Students learn more when questions are posed one at a time.

Application to CBT

    Lessons must require students to respond in some manner before the program will move on. Don't ask multiple questions at one time, or two or more questions in a sequence (except, of course, on quizzes and tests).

Principle 13

Students learn more when instructional feedback on the correctness of their work is provided.

Application to CBT

    Lessons must not only provide praise for correct answers but also must be individualized enough to explain why an incorrect answer doesn't work. A simple "Yes" or "No" is not sufficient for students to learn from their mistakes.

Principle 14

Students learn more when sustaining feedback is provided after an incorrect response (or no response) by probing, repeating the question, giving a clue, or allowing more time.

Application to CBT

Students should have more than one chance to answer a question. Programming should give clues about why an input is right or wrong and provide a hint to stimulate the thinking of the student toward getting the correct answer. Computers are infinitely patient and will wait until a student inputs an answer; they can also be programmed to prompt a student for an input after a preset amount of time. They do not (and should not), however, move on before a student attempts to answer.

Principle 15

Students learn more effectively when they are motivated by the material.

Application to CBT

Lessons must be designed to create and hold students' interest. Information must be presented in a manner that is deemed relevant to students and that shows them the reason why they need to know the material.

Principle 16

Students learn more effectively when the concepts taught are closely related to the real world.

Application to CBT

Lessons should provide practice that closely simulates the actual conditions under which the task will have to be performed. Simulation practices must be included in materials rather than just providing information. Even showing and telling is not enough — students must "do."

SUMMARY

Adult students don't move faster because they are adults, the move faster because of good instruction. When the instructional needs of any group are met, they progress. This principle holds true for everyone from pre-schoolers to adults; from the gifted to the educationally challenged.

Adults have the advantage over children in that they can come up to speed more rapidly in shorter periods of time on a topic because of their ability to process information faster with fewer examples. However, all learning is individual and personal; therefore, instruction should accommodate a variety of levels, styles, and rates.

CHAPTER 1-4
COST-EFFECTIVENESS OF CBT

INTRODUCTION

Cost is always a factor when considering any type of training. Few customers (either internal or external) have unlimited resources to develop what they really want. You will probably never encounter one! CBT does incur some front-end costs that traditional training does not — like investment in hardware and software development. However, the long-term costs have been shown to be cost-effective.

The Training and Development Journal carried an article in 1984 by Michael Hillelsohn in which he reported the results of a survey of 63 major corporations. Hillelsohn stated that although there was little quantitative evidence to support the assertions of those who responded, most companies who used CBT reported that it:

(1) improved job performance;
(2) reduced training time and cost;
(3) increased control and standardization of training; and
(4) successfully accomplished the decentralization of training.

Part of your job as a professional courseware designer is to educate customers on all aspects of a course and the ramifications of doing or not doing certain things. Your customer may only be looking at a snapshot — the immediate issue — "I need to solve a problem!" The customer may not be aware, for example, of the impact of delivering training or the legal issues of labor relations.

Of course, if you don't approach this correctly — from the aspect of what the customer needs to do to protect his or her company — it will come off as if you are just trying to increase the price of the project, or the amount of your own budget as an internal group. A sound rationale will help you educate your customer and sell your ideas.

WHAT TO DO

Costing a Project For a Customer

There are many terms for the document you provide your customer to cost a project: Request for Proposal (RFP), specifications document, proposal, letter of intent, bid, solicitation. A formal RFP is usually not required for internal customers; however, you will probably need to prepare some type of a proposal outlining what it is you intend to do and how much it will cost so that the customer knows what he or she will receive for the money spent. In most corporations, each department receives a training budget that it can spend as its needs require.

If the request that you must respond to:

(1) does not call for an evaluation,
(2) calls for levels of evaluation lower than you decide is required by the intended use of the course,
(3) requires that you bid a fixed price, or
(4) requires that you submit a compliant bid to specifications of the RFP, then

submit a compliant bid (or you will be eliminated on the first round). In addition, submit an alternate bid that provides the cost and rationale for the additional levels of evaluation. Even if the customer doesn't accept it, the alternate bid will have the additional benefit of protecting your company or internal group if there are any legal actions brought against the customer as a result of perceived or actual violations of Equal Employment Opportunity Commission (EEOC) fair testing practices. If your customer does accept the alternative proposal, everyone benefits.

If the RFP doesn't call for evaluation or you cannot convince your customer that the intended use of the course requires additional levels of evaluation, you should build in as much as possible so that the customer has a solid enough foundation to do further validation at the point where he or she realizes that it is needed. We recommend a minimum of content validity (explained fully in Unit 5, Evaluation).

Consortiums

Smaller businesses typically have fewer dollar resources to put into up-front development costs. This is where you might suggest the collaboration of a number of businesses with similar needs. In a consortium, several businesses contribute a certain amount of money over a period of time. At the end of that time, all of the contributors receive copies of the materials.

How To Do It

Costing

Develop your compliant bid to the specifications requested and submit it. Then present the alternate bid with the additional options you have determined will improve the training. Approach your customer with an explanation of the difference in the two prices and explain your rationale for why the higher cost is the most cost-effective over the long run. Most customers already have a pre-conceived idea of how much they can spend on the training. It is your job to help the customer satisfy his or her training needs — even if it means you have to recommend doing more or spending more money. The same applies if you think the customer could fulfill his or her training needs and achieve training objectives by spending *less*.

Consortiums

Through market research (which is a form of Needs Assessment) of businesses in a certain geographic area (best because a common location eliminates the need for travel), you can determine if there are similar needs among various businesses. You should probably look for businesses that are not in competition with each other so that consortium members do not lose any competitive advantage through sharing their ideas with others in the same business.

Once you identify the common need, bring the leaders of all of the groups together and explain the idea of the consortium. The benefits are:

(1) lower initial investment;
(2) investment amortized over a longer period of time; and
(3) everyone benefits from contributing a smaller amount of capital.

Once an agreement is reached, there are some things that must be worked out. You can't have direct input from *all* of the members of the consortium. The members must choose one person from among their own members empowered with final decision-making authority. The decision-making authority of this person is imperative. That way, your project will not get bogged down because the consortium members cannot agree.

You can lead the consortium into agreeing to terms and signing a contract. However, after that, the consortium meets on its own, discusses issues, and reviews designs and materials — only the decisions are brought back to you. Schedules become very important, and the members of the consortium must agree at the onset to adhere to them. Delays in decisions cannot be tolerated because they will harm everyone in the consortium.

RATIONALE

The objections to up-front investment can be overcome with the concept of the consortium. It is a feasible method in which all benefit.

Customers might think that they know what they want and explain their requirements very specifically. Although it is always wise to write a proposal that adheres to the specifications, if you think that you have a more feasible solution to the customer's problem, take the time to submit an alternate proposal. If the alternate proposal will cost less money, it will cause the customer to sit up and take notice. If the alternative will cost more, be sure that you have a very detailed rationale — or don't include the price of the alternate proposal until you have time to talk directly to the customer, explaining that although the costs may seem to be higher, the firm is actually realizing cost savings.

Those who control the purse strings on budgets understand the "bottom line" above all other rationales. If you simply turn in an alternate proposal with a higher sticker price, customers will look at the line beside "TOTAL" and reject the alternate on the spot.

There are three elements in any CBT project: quality, cost, and schedule (time). Reducing costs or shortening schedules reduces quality. This is illustrated in Figures 1-4-1 and 1-4-2.

Figure 1-4-1
Shortening Time of a Project and Its Effect on Quality

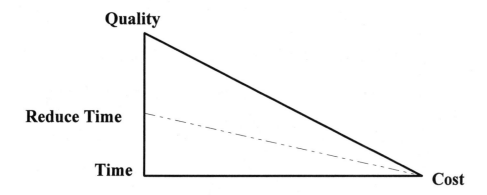

Figure 1-4-2
Reducing Cost of a Project and Its Effect on Quality

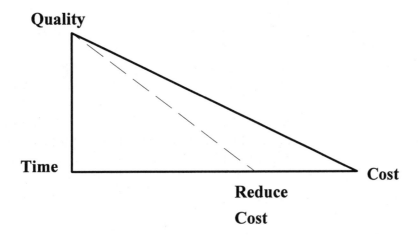

However, we do believe that it is possible to reduce the area of the triangle with effective formative evaluation strategies and quality control measures that reduce rework. This is illustrated in Figure 1-4-3. Reducing the overall area means reducing the cost of the project, making your company more competitive.

Figure 1-4-3
Effects of Quality Controls on Overall Project

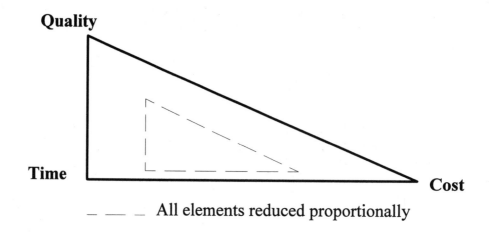

_ _ _ _ All elements reduced proportionally

CHAPTER 1-5
CONFIGURATION CONTROL

INTRODUCTION

This is not a book about project management but we have to say that planning is probably the most important factor in the success of your project. We have known many projects to founder on the rocks because of failure to adequately plan. There are two excellent books on project management (Greer, 1992; Bergman & Moore, 1990) that we refer you to for the management aspects of CBT projects. As we have stated in the Introduction to this book, there is no need to reinvent the wheel by attempting to repeat what has already been covered extremely well by other authors.

However, we are compelled to mention Configuration Control (CC) with respect to the review cycles that we recommend throughout each of the phases of a project. Configuration Control (and Review Cycles, covered in Chapter 3-6) are the quality controls of a project that obtain the superior results from CBT in terms of design and instruction.

WHAT TO DO

You must have a Configuration Control (CC) process that regulates the version of the materials under design, development, or review. Each team member must have access to the same configured version of the materials when different people are working on the same material.

HOW TO DO IT

You can make the CC process as complicated or as simple as you wish. Complicated procedures will slow down the process but provide more control. An important point is that a process is only as good as the people who use it. The team members must commit to follow the procedures in the process to ensure uniformity. Figure 1-5-1 outlines an example of a CC process that you might use.

The master copy of each version of the materials under development or review always remains archived. In that way, if electronic disks are corrupted while in use, you only lose changes back to the last archived version. Plus, you have the hard copy comments from the last version. It may be annoying to rework the material but at least the work is recoverable rather than lost forever.

This procedure continues until there is no need to return the lesson materials to the author and the materials can be stored by CC as the final version. The material is resurrected when entering the next phase of the project. Materials are then turned over to the next person in the process, who will make his or her contributions.

All project members must provide version copies of their electronic files to the CC designee for security. The CC designee is responsible for dispensing the correct version of the materials.

RATIONALE

Controlling the version of your materials in design, development, and review is critical to eliminating costly rework. When there is more than one person contributing to the same material, whether through reviews or during development, it is important that everyone have access to the same (latest) version of the materials. The important thing is to *have* a CC plan and to devise strategies for its implementation ahead of time. You will save yourself a lot of time that would otherwise be lost when you discover that various project team members are using different versions of the same material that is on disk or on a network.

APPLICATION TOOLS

The following outline is one way to effect Configuration Control over the materials that are in design, development, or review. It is not the only way. You should develop a CC method that fits your purposes and uses.

Figure 1-5-1
Configuration Control Process

Responsible Person or Department	Step

Author	1. Deliver the material to be reviewed to CC.
	
	  a. The electronic disk version should have a label indicating;
	    • the name of the document;
	    • the version of the document;
	    • the original author;
	    • the date of the version.
	
	  b. The hard copy version of the document should have the same information that is on the disk with the version number and date printed in the footer.

CC	2. Prepare the material for routing through the review cycle.
	
	  a. Make a duplicate of the material (soft and/or hard copy).
	
	  b. Label the original of the material as "Master Version 1" and the copy "Copy Version 1."
	
	  c. File the Master 1 of the material and circulate the Copy 1 for review.
	
	  d. Attach a routing sheet to each document that is put into review. The routing sheet should contain:
	    • the name of the document;
	    • the version of the document;
	    • a place for reviewers to sign their names and the date they completed the review;
	    • a place for final signoff if the document needs no changes.
	
	  e. Deliver the material to the first reviewer in the review cycle.

Reviewers	3. Complete one entire review cycle before the document goes back to the author for changes.
	4. The last reviewer returns the material to CC.

        NOTE: The first review should be the Technical Review. If the content contains significant technical inaccuracies, this reviewer can return the material to CC to send it back to the author for changes before completing the review cycle. This is the only reviewer who has this option. The reason for permitting this option for the technical reviewer is simple. If the material does contain significant inaccuracies, it will have to go through an entire review cycle again after the author makes the revisions. Therefore, it makes sense to cut down review time and cycles by catching these technical problems immediately.

CC	5. Return material to author.
Author	6. When the author gets the document back from review, he or she:

    a. opens the electronic document;

    b. makes changes to the document;

    c. saves it as Version 2;

    d. returns the original and Version 2 to CC.

CC	7. Prepare the material for routing through the second review cycle.

    a. Make a duplicate of the revised material (soft copy or hard copy).

    b. Label the original of the material as "Master Version 2" and the copy "Copy Version 2."

    c. File the Master 2 of the material and circulate the Copy 2 for review.

    d. Attach a routing sheet (same type as in Step 2d) to each document that is put into review. The routing sheet should contain:

- the name of the document;
- the version of the document;
- a place for reviewers to sign their names and the date they completed the review;
- a place for final signoff if the document needs no changes.

e. Deliver the material to the first reviewer in the review cycle.

Reviewers

8. Complete the second review cycle.

   a. It is important to note that second and subsequent review cycles are only to determine if all changes were made to the reviewer's satisfaction and for final signoff.

   b. If all changes were not made, initial that there are still changes to be made and pass it to the next reviewer.

   c. Last reviewer returns the material to CC.

CC

9. Return the material to the original author if there are still changes to be made. If all changes have been incorporated and the document is final CC, should mark the material as "Final Version" and file the material.

Author

10. If the material must go back to the author again, he or she:

    a. opens the electronic document;

    b. makes changes to the document;

    c. saves it as Version 3;

    d. returns Version 3 and 2 to CC.

[Cycles continue until there are no further changes required.]

Unit 1 References

> These are specific references for the chapters in this unit. For additional resources on topics in this unit, see the Bibliography.

Chapter 1-2

Floyd, S., Floyd, B., Hon, D., McEntee, P., O'Bryan, K., & Schwarz, M. (1982). *Handbook of Interactive Video*. White Plains, NY: Knowledge Industry Publications.

Milheim, W., Editor. (1994). *Authoring-Systems Software for Computer-Based Training*. Englewood Cliffs, NJ: Educational Technology Publications.

United States Air Force (Contract Number F41689-84-C-0012). *Nonpersonnel Studies and Analysis Service for Assessment of New Training Technologies*. Volume 1. United States Government.

Chapter 1-3

Lee, W. (1990). Bridging the Gap with IVD. *Training and Development Journal*, 44 (3), pp. 63-65.

Lillie, D., Hannum, W., & Stuck, G. (1989). *Computers and Effective Instruction*. New York: Longman.

Chapter 1-4

Fletcher, J. (1990). *Effectiveness and Cost of Interactive Videodisc Instruction in Defense Training and Education*. Alexandria, Virginia: Institute for Defense Analysis.

Hillelsohn, M. (1984). How to Think About CBT. *Training and Development Journal*, 38(2), pp. 42-44.

Meanor, D. & Lee, W. (1989). Private Sector/Public Sector Consortium Creates a "Teacher Induction" Interactive Videodisc Program. *Interactive Instruction Delivery*. Proceedings of the Seventh Conference of The Society for Applied Learning Technology (SALT): Orlando, Florida, pp. 44-46.

Chapter 1-5

Bergman, R. & Moore, T. (1990). *Managing Interactive Video/Multimedia Projects*. Englewood Cliffs, NJ: Educational Technology Publications.

Greer, M. (1992). *ID Project Management: Tools and Techniques for Instructional Designers and Developers*. Englewood Cliffs, NJ: Educational Technology Publications.

UNIT 2

Assessment/Analysis

Shandra performs an observation of Ginger's computer keyboard skills during Task Analysis using a valid observation instrument designed for the CBT project on teaching computer skills. Ginger is highly skilled in this area and the purpose is to determine the approach that makes her so efficient.

INTRODUCTION

It's a new day, your computer is humming, the database is loaded, and you are ready to go. You want to get your project off the ground so that you can start solving your customer's problem. First, however, you need to decide where to start: verify what the problem is, what is causing it, and select the most effective methodology to use in solving it. There are procedures available that will help you do this as effectively and as efficiently as a road map will help you find your way to a selected destination. They are:

1. **Needs Assessment** – A systematic way of exploring and establishing the type of solution needed.

2. **Front-end Analysis** – A collection of techniques that can be used in various combinations to help you narrow down the type and level of training or other intervention that will be required.

When you use a road map to decide how to get to your destination, you must first identify the starting place. The Assessment/Analysis Phase is that starting place in the ISD process. In addition, you must know the direction you need to go. The map identifies the route and all other delimiters for successful arrival at your destination or goal, that is, successful CBT.

In this phase you will:
- identify a broad range of goals;
- identify discrepancies between goals and strategies in use;
- identify priorities for action;
- summarize Assessment and Analysis data in an Analysis Report; and
- identify and write objectives for your training goals.

To help you complete these tasks, we present a number of Assessment and Analysis procedures and techniques from which you can select those most appropriate for your work. Each will be covered in a chapter of this Unit. An accompanying tool that will prove most useful as you proceed through these procedures and techniques is an electronic database with flexible fields. This database tool will enable you to store data from each of the analyses that you perform for later manipulation. These data will then roll up into your Analysis Report.

To avoid duplication, application tools with dual uses and which are described in detail in other Units have simply been referenced in this Unit.

Unit Content

We have chosen to use Chapter 2-1 to cover the techniques and tools you will use to gather Assessment and Analysis information. We feel that positioning these various tools first will help you select those that are most appropriate for your situation as you consider the various Assessment and Analysis procedures available.

This Unit will cover:

1. **Assessment/Analysis Instruments and Strategies**
   Self-completion Questionnaires
   Direct Interviews
   Focus Groups
   Direct Observation

26

2. Needs Assessment
   Underlying Assumptions
   Procedures
   Indicators for Using CBT

3. Audience Analysis
   Scope
   Procedures
   Indicators for Using CBT

4. Extant Data Analysis
   Scope
   Procedures
   Indicators for Using CBT

5. Situational Analysis
   Scope
   Procedures
   Indicators for Using CBT

6. Task Analysis
   Scope
   Procedures
   Indicators for Using CBT

7. Critical Incident Analysis
   Scope
   Procedures
   Indicators for Using CBT

8. Instructional Analysis
   Scope
   Procedures
   Indicators for Using CBT

9. Subject Matter Analysis
   Scope
   Procedures
   Indicators for Using CBT

10. Objective Analysis
   Objective Hierarchy
   Learning Domains
   Technical vs. Soft Skills
   Indicators for Using CBT

CHAPTER 2-1
ASSESSMENT/ANALYSIS INSTRUMENTS AND STRATEGIES

INTRODUCTION

Many times you will find that your customer has already conducted a Needs Assessment of the current situation. If this is true, you need to get that information so that you can incorporate it into the "big picture." You may also find that your customer has already decided on the solution and the delivery system for that solution. And, while the customer's Assessment may be quite thorough, it may also be flawed. Customers often think that the solution to a performance problem must be training. They may have only examined one aspect of their problem, missing the real cause, and losing any hope for an effective solution that remains hidden from their view.

Even if the customer's Assessment has valid and reliable results, with training areas selected, you still need to map out a strategy and methodology to collect information about the proposed training. The instruments and strategies that you use to conduct Assessment and Analysis must meet two criteria. They must:

(1) have internal consistency/validity (content validity); and
(2) demonstrate reliability (interrater agreement).

Data-gathering instruments that are hastily constructed, not validated, and not reliable will produce inaccurate information, and training development will be off target from the writing of objectives onward. Procedures to establish validity and reliability are explained in Unit 5, Evaluation.

After all data is gathered, how do you decide to use CBT? We have included a section at the end of each chapter in this unit on the indicators derived from each type of assessment or analysis that would point to the use of CBT as the solution to the training problem.

WHAT TO DO

Types of Instruments

There are four main types of data gathering methods that require different instruments. These methods are:

(1) self-completion questionnaires;
(2) direct interviews;
(3) focus groups; and
(4) direct observation.

The methods for developing questionnaires are discussed in Unit 5, Evaluation. The strategies to use in collecting information using these instruments are discussed here.

Self-Completion Questionnaires

Questionnaires are an effective way to gain information from a large sample of a population. Questions must be constructed properly. Poorly constructed questionnaires allow for wide interpretation by each person who completes one, and therefore provide little valuable information. Constructing useful questionnaires and establishing Content Validity for questionnaires is covered in Unit 5, Evaluation.

Questionnaires are limited in that they only provide the information requested. This limitation can be exacerbated if questionnaires are returned anonymously. In that case there is no way to contact respondents if their answers deviate greatly from the responses of the rest of the sample. It would be valuable to know what unique experiences caused them to respond the way they did. One way around this particular difficulty is to send out confidential instead of anonymous questionnaires.

Of course, those questionnaires that are intended to be anonymous should remain anonymous. Because this makes it impossible for you to follow-up with your respondents, you should carefully consider your options before selecting anonymity.

Direct Interviews

During Needs Assessment, direct interviews are often used to gather information on job-related needs. The procedures for constructing instruments and conducting interviews listed here apply to both the Assessment and Evaluation Phases.

Interviews have four advantages:

(1) They are a direct link to persons who have unique information about the problem you are investigating.
(2) They are structured by the elements of schedule and planning; contain specific rules, and have a specific focus.
(3) They allow for the collection of immediate follow-up information.
(4) The results are analyzed.

NOTE: Although this section focuses on structured interviews, don't overlook valuable information that might come out in informal conversations with individuals. Anything you hear or read may be useful later. Take notes, organize your information, and remember to review it as you proceed with your assessment and analyses.

Focus Groups

If job descriptions and prerequisite skills are not accurate, focus groups should be convened to develop a job description and list of prerequisite skills that accurately reflect the position and the job holder. A focus group consists of current job holders and their supervisors, convened separately or jointly to determine the knowledge, skills, and attitudes (KSA) required of the job holder.

Direct Observation

Sometimes it is not convenient or practical to collect job-related information in a situation that is removed from where the work will actually be carried out. In these cases, a simple, yet effective, method of collecting information is direct observation.

How To Do It •

Gathering Information Through Self-Completion Questionnaires

If questionnaires are sent out confidentially, a number code system should be developed that can trace a specific questionnaire to a list of names to help retrieve this potentially valuable information. Make sure, however, that you inform all respondents that the confidentiality of their responses will be strictly observed.

Once you construct the questions you want to ask, have them approved by management or the customer's designee with authority to make decisions on the project. There may be some information that you are not allowed to ask because of labor union agreements or governmental regulations. (See Unit 5, Evaluation for detailed information on constructing questionnaires.) Provide your customer with a written plan that details how you will conduct the surveys, select participants, assure anonymity, and analyze and report the information.

It is very optimistic to expect to get a 50% return rate on surveys. Here is a way to ensure that you get the total number of responses you need. Keep this 50% return rate in mind and use the same formula and method for sample size and random selection interviewees when choosing subjects who will receive surveys. Proceed as follows:

a. You have a list of 500 names.
b. Sample size of 10% of the population means you need 50 responses.

c. Anticipating a 50% return rate, double the number of names (total 100).

d. You derive a random sample of 100 names who receive the survey.

e. Re-send the survey to those non-respondents from the **same** group if you don't get the 50 you need on the first try.

f. If you still do not get the required number after the second time, repeat from step **c** with a **different** group.

g. Use all responses (the 50 required is a minimum; more than that is even better).

Gathering Information Through Direct Interviews

The interviewer must prepare for the interviews, maintain control during the interviews, and analyze the results of the interviews.

Preparation includes studying any available handbooks and dictionaries to learn the jargon of the people you will be interviewing, developing questionnaires for interviews, and presenting the questionnaires to the customer for final approval.

Selecting Interviewees

Once the interview questions are approved by management, the next step is to choose the persons to be interviewed. Often customers want to provide you with a list of hand-selected persons to interview. Discourage them from this hand-selection because these persons might not represent a random sample of the population being investigated, but rather might be persons who are generally perceived positively by management. Request a list of all persons who are among the population to be interviewed. Randomly select names based on the total number of names on the list, divided by twice the number of interviewees desired for the sample. For example:

> If you are given a list with 1000 names and wish to have a 10 percent sample (100 interviewees), you need to select 200 names — every fifth name on the list — from which you will select a random sample. These calculations are:

> **1000 × .10 = 100 (desired sample)**
> **100 × 2 = 200 (random sample size)**
> **1000 ÷ 200 = 5 (every fifth name)**

Continue calling persons on the derived list until you have scheduled the desired number of persons to interview (in the example above, call until you have commitments from 100 people).

If the customer insists on hand-selecting those persons who will be interviewed, explain the drawbacks to this type of selection process, but abide by his or her wishes. However, you should note the selection process in the Analysis Report.

A confidentiality agreement must be made with the customer, in writing, to show to interviewees. This will assure them of the anonymity of their responses and make them more open to "give you the facts." We have included an example in the Application Tools section of this chapter.

When calling potential interviewees, you will need to explain what the purpose of the interview is and enlist their cooperation. During this contact, explain:

(1) the purpose of the interview;
(2) their role in the interview;
(3) the confidential nature of the interview;
(4) how the information collected in the interview will be used and who will receive the data; and
(5) the potential impact on the organization.

Scheduling Interviews

Consider all the following factors when scheduling interviews:

1. Schedule a specific time and place for the interviews.
2. Leave a 30 to 45 minute break between interviews (if they will not be tape recorded).
3. Don't schedule interviews before lunch or late in the day.
4. Make appointments directly with the interviewee rather than leaving messages.
5. Avoid lunch interviews.
6. Be present when the interviewee arrives.
7. Conduct the interviews in a neutral location.

Starting the Interview

Don't begin questioning immediately. First, put the interviewee at ease by explaining the purpose of the interview again. Second, show the interviewee the confidentiality statement from management. Third, ask the interviewee if he or she objects to having the session tape recorded.

Explain that tape recording helps get all of the information exactly as the interviewee expresses it and eliminates the need to interpret notes later, thus omitting important points. Very few persons will object to having the session tape recorded. However, if they do object, you will have to slow the pace of the interview to get the detailed information through notes.

Conducting the Interview

After establishing rapport with the interviewee, begin the interview. Here are some suggestions for making the interview successful:

1. Arrange the room comfortably for the interview. Sit opposite the person interviewed so that eye contact is possible but avoid putting a desk or table

between yourself and the interviewee. A table or desk puts up a subtle barrier that might influence the interview results. Rather, put two chairs on either side of a low, small table that can hold the tape recorder. Be certain that the table has a pad or cover so that if the table is used to set drinks (offer the interviewee a beverage) or papers on, there will be little audio distortion.

2. Focus your attention on the interviewee, don't let your mind wander. You might want to question an interviewee further on a particular statement.

3. Sequence questions from general to specific. Ask for concrete examples about statements made, ask key questions in more than one way, and rephrase questions that the interviewee does not understand.

4. Ask for constructive criticism but keep the criticism focused on the problem, not specific people. Don't encourage long discourses on what appears to be private gripes. Use the next question on the questionnaire to ask for a specific example to refocus the interview.

5. Ask if the opinions expressed by the interviewee are held generally through the organization or whether they are his or her views alone.

6. Admit an error if you make one.

7. Avoid disagreeing with the interviewee as well as expressing sarcasm, correcting, and contradicting. If you find yourself in a personality conflict or a power struggle, simply terminate the interview.

8. Don't bring the interview to a stop abruptly. Conclude the interview by summarizing the points made by the interviewees and thank them for their time and the valuable information they provided.

Remember, one-to-one interviews are expensive in terms of time and money. A well-structured interview will minimize the use of both while still gaining the maximum amount of information.

Interviewer Skills

Above all, when personally interviewing someone, be a good listener. Remember, you are present to learn. Don't monopolize the talk. There are certain skills that good interviewers must have:

Initiate	Use questions and statements to get the session going and keep it moving.
Regulate	Pace the session by periodically summarizing or, if necessary, pointing out time restrictions.
Inform	Clarify/provide information that the interviewee or group[4] might not know.

---

[4]Group is also used here because the interviewer needs these same skills when conducting group interviews or focus groups (discussed later).

Support	Discourage the interviewee from attacking the viewpoints of the organization or other members of the group. Regularly remind each interviewee or group member that the purpose of the session is to get his or her point of view, not a critique of the views of others.
Evaluate	Provide a reality check by reflecting back to the interviewee or group, in summary form, what has been stated.

Gathering Information Through Focus Groups

Focus Groups will normally be organized by the customer, who will provide both the space and the employees who will attend the sessions. This is usually done at the customer's discretion, but you might want to request that the customer keep the following considerations in mind when selecting focus group members:

1. Members should be those who are considered exemplary workers by their supervisors and peers.
2. If the position is being newly created, supervisors who will work with the job holder should participate in writing the job description to delineate what KSAs will be needed to successfully fill that position.
3. Members should be assigned rather than volunteer. This will help ensure that you get a representative sample of the members of the work group. Volunteers will sometimes have their own agenda that precipitates their desire to participate. Personal agendas of members of the focus group, while they often generate a lot of debate, are counterproductive to the purpose of the session. If the volunteer is highly verbal, has a strong personality, and is very persuasive, he or she might actually dominate the session, which will skew the results of the focus group and not accurately represent the description of the job holder.

Conducting Focus Groups

There are several techniques used for conducting focus groups; some requiring and some not requiring consensus. What has worked best for us is using a technique that does not require consensus of the focus group members. This seems to foster discussion and information exchange better than those techniques that require consensus. It is, however, important to prioritize the items in order of relative importance across the entire group. We use a Rank and Order (RAO) technique.

With large numbers of items (duties, etc.), the first RAO might be conducted to arrange the items within some logical structure.

Follow these steps in conducting an RAO:

1. Provide a random list of items to be considered by each focus group member.

2. Request that each member individually prioritize each item in the list in order of importance from 1 to *n* (however many items are in the list).
3. Chart each member's prioritized number of each of the items on the list.
4. Sum the group's responses and divide by the number of responses.
5. Rewrite the list in the prioritized format, with numbers closer to 1 at the top, indicating that they were considered more important.
6. Look for large gaps in the totals that might be natural breaking points for high-to-medium-to-low-priority items.
7. Discuss the highest priority items with the focus group members and get expressions of why each item has high priority. Ask those members who did not give a high rank to those items to voice their reasons for the lower priority. Their reasoning might be due to a misinterpretation of the statement, or the reasoning might change the opinions of others in the group regarding the relative position of an item. Follow the same procedure for low-priority items. Eliminate any items the group agrees do not belong.
8. Repeat steps 2 through 5.

The resulting list should be the group's estimate of the requirements for successful performance on the job.

Gathering Information Through Observation

You should select a subject matter expert (SME) to observe, and write down everything that the person performing the job does. Observations may be made in-person or be videotaped for later observation. Your job is to develop a behavioral description that consists of the inputs from the observed behavior, actions, and outputs. When collecting information through observations, following these steps will be helpful:

1. Identify team members who will conduct the observations.
2. Develop observation checklists using the recommended techniques of validity in Unit 5, Evaluation.
3. Train observers using the recommended techniques of reliability in Unit 5, Evaluation.
4. Identify exemplary (successful) job performers to be observed.
5. Request permission for observations and provide dates and times.
6. Ensure that your observations are as unobtrusive as possible.
7. Mark the checklist but take a minimum of additional notes.[5]
8. Share observations with the job performers (if appropriate).[6]

---

[5] Excessive note taking (if the observer can be seen by the subject observed) can make the subject nervous or self-conscious, which might affect performance.

[6] An example of an inappropriate time to share information would be if the subject will be observed on subsequent occasions. The fact that information will or will not be shared and the frequency of the sharing should be clarified with the subject prior to the first observation.

Analyzing Information

Assessment/Analysis is one form of evaluation and many of the techniques used here apply in evaluation as well. Analyzing information from the methods listed above is fully discussed in Unit 5, Evaluation.

RATIONALE

Getting enough of the right information can be critical to the success, in terms of both cost and training outcomes, of your CBT project. Starting your development journey with the right information will ensure that your specifications will scope out the problem, and that your solution accurately provides for your customer visible and measurable successes in achieving important training goals.

APPLICATION TOOLS

Refer to Unit 5, Evaluation for examples of application tools that can be used to collect data. Figure 2-1-1 is an example of a confidentiality agreement.

Figure 2-1-1
Confidentiality Agreement Form

(On Customer Letterhead)

I *(name of customer representative)*, as a representative of *(customer's organizational name)*, agree that the information gained from the participation of company employees in the *(insert project name)* training project will remain strictly confidential and that individual performance or scores need not be divulged to the company. Individual information will be known solely to *(your name or organization)* whose representatives will guard that data with strictest security.

Only cumulative results of assessment studies or analyses will be divulged to the company in the form of a final report.

_____

Signature of Customer Representative

_____

Date

_____

Signature of *(your name/organization)*

_____

Date

CHAPTER 2-2
NEEDS ASSESSMENT

INTRODUCTION

Needs Assessment is the systematic process of determining goals, identifying discrepancies between actual and desired conditions, and establishing priorities for action (Lee & Roadman, 1991). Needs Assessment is accomplished by developing Assessment questionnaires; establishing procedures for collecting data, such as mailings, telephone, and personal interviews; analyzing data to produce meaningful information.

Needs Assessment can be done at any level from a specific job to a division or department and even entire organizations. But, in the ISD Process for CBT, it most often applies to the program or course level.

Gagné, Briggs, and Wager (1988) identified five types of needs:

1. Normative

A need that is compared to a standard.

Example #1: Industry standards establish that it should take 750 hours of development time for each hour of CBT delivery. Company X currently takes 1500 hours to do this so it needs to find ways to reduce its time to meet this standard in order to bid competitively.

Example #2: Bank A might not be as competitive as Bank B in offering a wide variety of services to customers because they are not automated enough to efficiently process the paperwork required to deliver those services. Bank A needs automation to bring it to the same level as Bank B.

2. Felt

What people think they need.

Example: The executives of a sales and marketing firm believe that their sales representatives need training in interpersonal relations because they don't share valuable information that could help others increase their sales. They feel a need for this training to solve their problem.

3. Expressed/Demand   Supply and demand.

Example: Insurance Company Y is looking for ways to improve the speed of processing claims because a private consulting company delivered the results of a survey it conducted showing that motorists use this as the number one criteria in selecting a company to insure with.

4. Comparative Need   Some people have a particular attribute; others don't.

Example: Retailer A finds that its customer service representatives resolve customer inquires on an average of 10 resolutions per measurement unit. The range between representatives, however, is from 5 to 15 resolutions. The retailer needs to bring all customer service representatives to a maximum level of efficient processing while maintaining customer satisfaction.

5. Anticipated/Future   Projected demands.

Example: A steering committee of Bank A has decided that for it to be competitive it must automate additional functions to provide more services to its customers. They state this fact in their five-year strategic plan.

Underlying Assumptions

Once needs are assessed, there is occasionally the temptation to think the job is done and to apply a time-honored solution to the problem — training. Keep in mind, however, that:

1. Training is not the solution to every problem. Companies that believe training is always the solution to a problem are going down the rosy path to destruction. Let's consider the example of the felt need listed above. After analysis of the problem, the sales and marketing firm might realize that their representatives keep information to themselves rather than share it with fellow representatives because the company's merit raise policy, company trips, and other perquisites are based on individual sales volume. If the company wants representatives to share information so that all benefit, they simply need to change company policy. As long as present policy exists, no amount of training is going to convince high-achieving sales representatives that they should share information that will better able others to compete with them.

2. Assessment must be conducted thoroughly, without bias, and with forethought. Simply looking at one side of an issue or problem, or from the perspective of one or a small group of individuals, will probably not yield answers that are accurate.

3. The individuals sampled must be a representative cross-section of all persons affected by the issue, who listen to their colleagues, and don't follow their own personal agenda.

WHAT TO DO

Basic Steps

There are four steps in conducting a Needs Assessment. They are:

1. Identify the broad range of goals — what knowledge and skills are needed to successfully complete the work.
2. Rank the goals in order of importance — show dependencies.
3. Identify discrepancies between expected and actual performance required to meet a goal — list all discrepancies as well as missing tasks.
4. Set priorities for action — set these against the backdrop of the job goals, desired results, and other relevant factors.

How To Do It

A customer will identify a problem and come to you for help with the solution. The following steps outline the procedures you can follow to conduct a comprehensive and effective Needs Assessment:

A. Define the Problem
   1. You must identify the knowledge and skills needed to perform the task. Any of the data collection techniques outlined in Chapter 2-1 can be used to do this.
   2. Identify the job-specific knowledge and skill areas used to select persons for the job. These can be identified when you conduct step one.
   3. Is there a match?
      • *YES* – look to environmental causes of the problem. Go to 5 and then step E.
      • *NO* – identify the tasks that are missing. Go to 4.
   4. Review missing tasks for possible training applications.
   5. Visit the work environment. Look for task performance affected by the following. List all that apply.
      • Noise
      • Speed
      • Equipment
      • Tools
      • Temperature

- Ventilation
6. Create a questionnaire that addresses issues that employees may have in areas such as:
   - Management support
   - Teamwork
   - Empowerment
   - Safety
   - Job knowledge
7. Review all results and identify areas of need (refer to the needs and examples listed).

B. Define the job goals and compare them with the results of your Assessment in step A.

C. List all possible solutions suggested by the Assessment. You will be surprised by how often training is not a solution suggested by your Assessment. If it is on your list, identify the impact that not providing the training (selecting another way to solve the problem) will have on performance goals.

D. Define the impact of each solution in terms of time, money, and customer satisfaction.

E. Make recommendations.

F. Begin Front-end Analysis.

INDICATORS FOR USING CBT

The indicators from the various types of Needs Assessment that would indicate CBT is a viable option for the delivery of the training are:

1.	Normative Need	If the industry as a whole is presently using computerized systems in the area of training.
2.	Felt Need	If the management who are funding the project feels that there is a need for the training to be CBT.
3.	Expressed or Demand Need	If the company needs to be computerized in order to be more competitive and maintain or increase its market share.
4.	Comparative Need	If other people who hold similar jobs to those who will receive the training have computer skills.
5.	Anticipated/Future Need	If experts feel that the trend in the industry for which the training is designed is going to move toward computerization.

RATIONALE

Needs Assessment is an important first step in the life of your project. Creating instruction for which there is no need is both costly and foolish. A thorough

Needs Assessment will establish whether or not training is needed. And, when training is the need, Needs Assessment will help pinpoint the type and duration of training best suited to meet that need.

NOTE: CBT is not always the answer, just as training is not!

Always keep in mind a simple, but frequently forgotten, rule of thumb: "don't declare a solution before you identify the problem and its causes." This rule of thumb can be used to summarize the rationale for well-designed and implemented Assessment and Analysis. Training development companies and internal teams will come under increasing criticism for developing training that "misses the mark" if they do not adhere to sound Assessment/Analysis practices.

Many training development companies and internal training staffs accept exactly what the customer gives them and set to work developing what the customer wants, or thinks he/she wants, without exercising professional judgment and informing the customer that there might be an alternative solution. It is rare to hear of anyone attempting to convince a customer of an alternative solution that might be less expensive or even to suggest that the solution is not training.

However, losing one contract or assignment might bring many more contracts, along with the respect of a customer who sees the integrity and professionalism of a training development team. Delivering a training product that shouldn't have been developed to begin with might result in the loss of many more contracts from that customer, even though the product was the result of the customer's own Needs Assessment and Analysis.

Remember, customers come to you because of your expertise and professionalism. It is your responsibility to provide guidance so that your customers get what they really need, not just what they asked for!

APPLICATION TOOLS

Use the Needs Assessment summary in Figure 2-2-1 to report the results of your Needs Assessment.

Figure 2-2-1
Needs Assessment Summary

1. **Statement of the problem:**

2. **Data collection methods used:**

3. **Data analysis:**

   Job goals:

   Potential solutions:

4. **Recommendations:**

CHAPTER 2-3
AUDIENCE ANALYSIS

INTRODUCTION

Once Needs Assessment determines that training is required, the next step is to determine exactly *what* training is needed. This is done by using the tools of Front-end Analysis to collect and analyze all relevant data regarding a problem. The analysis tools, and the distinctions between them, that we will examine in the remainder of this unit are:

1.	Audience Analysis	Identifying the background and some of the learning characteristics of the potential students with respect to the job they will have to perform.
2.	Extant Data Analysis	Identifying existing training materials, manuals, references, and syllabi.
3.	Situational Analysis	Identifying possible environmental/organizational constraints that may have an impact on training goals and design.
4.	Task Analysis	A detailed description of the job-related tasks that the worker must perform after completing the training.
5.	Critical Incident Analysis	Identifying the tasks that require training.
6.	Instructional Analysis	Identifying the learning characteristics of the target audience. This includes prerequisite skills.
7.	Subject Matter Analysis	Identifying the specific content related to a program that enables the designer to develop content appropriate for the audience level.
8.	Objective Analysis	Writing the objectives for the tasks that will be trained.

NOTE: Some consider Analyses 7 and 8 to be part of Design. That's OK.

Each of the Front-end Analysis tools build on others, so we recommend that you conduct your Analysis in the following order:

1. Analysis 2 can actually be done anytime before you begin to develop training.

2. Analyses 1 and 3 must be completed before Analysis 5 because they provide background information that will influence Analysis 5.
3. Analysis 4 must be done before Analysis 5 because you must know what all of the tasks are before you can select or de-select those to be trained.
4. Analysis 6 must be completed before Analyses 7 and 8 because it provides input into these two analyses in that the results of 6 feed into the type and amount of training you need to deliver.
5. Analyses 7 and 8 can be done in either order.

You may not conduct every analysis listed for every project. The requirements of the project will determine which to use and which can be omitted.

WHAT TO DO

Sitting through a training session that teaches something you already know must rank high on everyone's list of least favorite experiences. Audience Analysis is a tool that you use to identify the background and some of the learning characteristics of your target training population.

Begin by analyzing the job descriptions that are usually available for positions within a company. These descriptions will generally or specifically detail the types of duties members of the audience for this training will perform. Job descriptions usually contain a "catch-all" phrase that will read something like "...and other duties as assigned." Be certain to identify if these other duties fall within or outside of the scope of the training that is to be developed. Generic descriptions can be verified (and modifications made) using data collected during interviews or observation.

The current status of the job description is a critical issue. If the job description was recently revised, it probably accurately reflects the duties of the persons who hold that position. If it is not current, you should determine its accuracy by speaking with customer representatives or contacts. The issue of accuracy is one that might well be raised in any case in a time of rapid change and growth in business and industry.

At a minimum, the job descriptions you analyze should contain the following:

(1) **Position Title** — The job name. This should be part of an overall organizational structure/hierarchy.
(2) **Position Description (Generic)** — A broad description or listing of the job actions/activities which are required for successful job performance.
(3) **Knowledge, Skills, Attitudes (KSA)** — A specific listing of the knowledge, skills, and attitudes required for successful job performance.
(4) **Proficiency Measures** — A listing and explanation of the performance measures used for the job tasks.

NOTE: If job descriptions do not exist for a position, they should be developed during the Needs Assessment.

How To Do It

From the job description, make a flowchart of the job, starting with the goal or product and working backward. Use this flowchart to identify any prerequisite job skills as well as all critical steps and their related skills in the job process.

Interview the incumbents (job performers) and their supervisors using the flowchart you have developed and verify that the flowchart of critical steps/skills (the job description) and list of prerequisite skills you have identified:

(1) accurately reflect their current duties;
(2) are the correct entry level skills for the job; and
(3) contain the current/projected number of incumbents (this will be needed when you look at training costs and materials production).

An alternative approach that you can use in the interview is to show the incumbents and supervisors a copy of the job descriptions and ask them:

(1) to interpret what each duty involves and if they believe they, or their work group members, can perform those duties; and
(2) to review your list of prerequisite skills and tell you if they believe they, or their work group members, have these skills.

Indicators For Using CBT

Indicators exist that CBT is a suitable method for delivering training, if the users of the training:
- are of sufficient numbers to cost-justify the training;
- are computer literate to some extent;
- have previously taken courses by computer;
- have a positive attitude toward CBT;
- are independent learners; and
- do not require human interaction for verification, clarification, and feedback.

Rationale

In addition to providing insights into the needs of your potential training audience, understanding the learning characteristics of your target audience will help you to apply the other analysis tools explained in this chapter. The characteristics that you identify through Audience Analysis are an important element in conducting an effective Task Analysis as well as providing you with an overall picture of what is needed as you conduct Subject Matter and Critical Incident Analyses.

APPLICATION TOOLS

Standard flowcharting or outlining techniques can be used to list any prerequisite job skills as well as all critical steps and their related skills. Keeping track of these (and your other Assessment and Analysis) data is facilitated greatly if you use a good commercial database management program. A flowchart example can be found in Chapter 3-4.

Audience Analysis information rolls up into the Analysis Report found in the Application Tools section of Chapter 2-9.

CHAPTER 2-4
EXTANT DATA ANALYSIS

INTRODUCTION

You are going to analyze training needs, so, what better place to look for the type of skills trained and the scope of that training than in existing materials? A search for what is available used to be a rather daunting task, but with advances in telecommunications and computer technology, this search, or Extant Data Analysis, has become relatively simple to complete and provides an added level of confidence and reliability for those who take the time to complete it.

WHAT TO DO

There are many sources of information to complete an Extant Data Analysis. The numerous guides and indexes to periodicals found in libraries are excellent first sources of information. Many libraries offer online computer searches of information on nearly any topic. The various clearinghouses of the Educational Resources Information Center (ERIC) provide computerized databases that are available at many colleges and universities. Information searches can be conducted using bulletin board services (BBS) and special interest groups on the Internet, provided you have an online account or access to one. Computerized data searches are also becoming available on more and more commercial online services. Search costs vary from a fixed fee per search to a charge per unit of search time and amount of information generated.

The key to successful Extant Data searches is the organization of the search. Pursuing a strategy of examining only shelved professional library periodicals that usually address the topic under development is not a complete, nor very efficient, method of conducting such a search. When developing questions for a computer search, write your question as narrowly as the topic can be defined. The computer searches on key words and can only give you back information based on what you put in.

Someone still has to *read* the articles once the data from the computer search are generated! Or someone has to go find the paper articles if the electronic search provides only a bibliography. Sometimes the time available for this review is limited, so reducing the amount of material that you have to review and collecting the most relevant data in the fastest way possible are critical.

Extant Data Analysis also includes the examination and evaluation of the suitability and possible use of existing training. The sources for this extant data are many—from training development houses, to advertisements, to vendors at professional conferences. There is no need to reinvent the wheel if the training already exists in an off-the-shelf version that can be purchased and adapted to meet a particular training need.

How To Do It

Your analysis should progress through the steps that follow. Do not be surprised if Step 6 does not produce significant results for you. If you find that you have suitable materials, proceed to Step 7. If you find that nothing remains that is suitable, proceed to Step 8.

Procedures:

1. Determine what it is that you are looking for. Is it information on an entire course, or on one or more tasks?
2. Identify likely sources:
   - Internal training resources
   - Professional organizations
   - Training vendors
   - Universities/schools
   - Library searches
   - Other commercial search facilities
   - Existing technical manuals
3. Gather information and/or course materials.
4. Compare materials/courseware with critical incidents (once determined).
5. Select the most relevant materials/courseware.
6. Determine the usability of the materials you have selected. Match materials for critical analysis, version availability, amount of extraneous information, potential for modification to your customer's needs, and cost of modification vs. development.
7. Make a decision to "buy" if the results of your analysis produce courseware that is usable as is (within your timeliness and cost guidelines) or can be modified to meet your customer's needs.
8. Make a decision to "develop" training materials if the results of your analysis do not produce usable or adaptable courseware.

INDICATORS FOR USING CBT

CBT is a viable solution for training if your Extant Data Analysis finds that:
- There are CBT courses already developed that can be used off-the-shelf (as they are) or can be modified to meet the customer's needs.
- No such CBT courses exist as yet, but you encounter news that other, respected, groups or companies are calling for CBT development in this area.

RATIONALE

Taking the time and expending the effort to conduct a thorough Extant Data Analysis can provide the information you need to make an informed decision on how best to use valuable time and resources to get the results your customer needs and wants.

APPLICATION TOOLS

The tools that you can use to conduct your Extant Data Analysis are drawn from the results of the Assessment. Again, we would like to stress the importance of having a flexible database management program that will allow you to categorize and manipulate the data you collect.

The increase in the sophistication of and wide availability of online data and search facilities has dramatically increased the amount of information that Extant Data Analysis can deliver. Examining their potential is outside the scope of this book. We have, however, provided several excellent references for those interested in examining this area further (see Bibliography at the end of this book).

Figure 2-4-1 is a form that you can use to record your findings during Extant Data Analysis.

Figure 2-4-1
Extant Data Analysis Form

1. Source of Information:

2. Type of Information:

Article____
Book____
Course Material____
User Manual____
Other____

3. Summary of Information Found:

4. Probability of Use:

Very low	Low	Moderate	High	Very High

| 1 | 2 | 3 | 4 | 5 |

CHAPTER 2-5
SITUATIONAL ANALYSIS

INTRODUCTION

If you actually observed the job being performed during your Needs Assessment, you may have noted the physical conditions in which the job is performed. If you didn't, taking the time to conduct a Situational Analysis can help you zero in on the environmental factors in the workplace that will impact job and task performance.

WHAT TO DO

Visiting the work environment is the best way to conduct a Situational Analysis. Any training that you develop will be designed to ensure successful job performance. Before you can be sure of what to put into this training, you need to examine the work environment for factors that detract from or enhance how successful an employee will be in performing specific, job-related tasks and the conditions under which training will have to be delivered.

Viewing videotapes of the work being done and the environment in which it is done will provide you some data, but will not allow you to question job performers "real-time" or experience some of the environmental factors that affect performance such as temperature, ventilation, etc. Also, with video, you can only see what the lens of the camera sees, not everything on the periphery.

HOW TO DO IT

Visit the place where the job is typically performed and look for task performance affected by the following:

- Noise
- Processing speed
- Equipment
- Tools
- Temperature
- Ventilation
- Other physical/environmental factors

Your next step is to confirm your observations. An effective method is to develop a questionnaire based on your observations and related situational issues that employees may have and to use this questionnaire to interview the job performers. Related situational issues could be in areas such as:

- Management Support
- Teamwork
- Empowerment
- Safety
- Job knowledge

INDICATORS FOR USING CBT

Indicators exist that CBT is an appropriate solution for training if your Situation Analysis reveals that:

- students are dispersed over a large geographical area, making it impractical to bring students to a central location;
- information must be dispersed to a large number of students in a short period of time;
- information needs to be delivered on an "as needed" basis over a long period of time rather than in large amounts over a short period of time; and
- students cannot be released from their jobs for a sufficient amount of time to attend classes.

RATIONALE

Taking the time at the beginning of your analysis to examine factors that affect job performance and training delivery will further ensure that your final design will be based on actual, rather than perceived, training needs. Meeting a customer's training needs is what good CBT design is intended to accomplish.

APPLICATION TOOLS

The questionnaire and interview guidelines discussed in Chapter 2-1 (including Focus Group Techniques) can be used in conducting a Situational Analysis. However, observation is the best method to collect data. See the work or training delivery environment yourself, first hand.

CHAPTER 2-6
TASK ANALYSIS

INTRODUCTION

Task Analysis is an outgrowth of Audience Analysis. Once the duties of the job holder are determined, the tasks within each duty must be defined. Within each task are the sub-tasks, or steps, necessary to complete the task.

We have placed Task Analysis before Critical Incident Analysis to help focus each of these phases. The focus of Task Analysis is on ascertaining all the job-related tasks. The focus of Critical Incident Analysis is on prioritizing and selecting those tasks that must be trained.

WHAT TO DO

A well-structured Task Analysis should follow the process represented in Figure 2-6-1 and provide you with the information that you need to construct a list of all the tasks required for successful completion of a specific job. The Task Analysis should:

(1) define the position;
(2) identify all job-related duties;
(3) identify all tasks; and
(4) identify all sub-tasks that support the identified tasks (KSAs).

HOW TO DO IT

The following steps outline the procedure to follow when conducting a Task Analysis:

1. Define the position. Identify:
    - The major job outputs.
    - Previous job/task analyses.
    - Impact on work environment.
    - Training to new or existing procedures or equipment.

    For example, a job might be "An Instructional Designer."

Figure 2-6-1 Task Analysis Flowchart

```
                              ┌──────────────┐
                              │     Job      │
                              └──────────────┘
          ┌──────────────┐  ┌──────────────┐  ┌──────────────┐
          │     Duty     │  │     Duty     │  │     Duty     │
          └──────────────┘  └──────────────┘  └──────────────┘

   ┌──────────┐   ┌──────────┐      ┌──────────┐   ┌──────────┐
   │   Task   │   │   Task   │      │   Task   │   │   Task   │
   └──────────┘   └──────────┘      └──────────┘   └──────────┘

  ┌─┐ ┌─┐ ┌─┐ ┌─┐  ┌─┐ ┌─┐     ┌─┐ ┌─┐ ┌─┐ ┌─┐   ┌─┐ ┌─┐
  │K│ │S│ │S│ │S│  │S│ │A│     │K│ │K│ │S│ │S│   │S│ │S│
  └─┘ └─┘ └─┘ └─┘  └─┘ └─┘     └─┘ └─┘ └─┘ └─┘   └─┘ └─┘
                                    ┌─┐ ┌─┐
                                    │S│ │A│
                                    └─┘ └─┘
```

K = Knowledge

S = Skill

A = Attitude

****

2. Identify all job-related duties.
   - Break the job into manageable groups which are, at this point, arbitrary.
   - Ensure each is independent of other duties.
   - Identify duties **before** tasks.

   For example, specific duties of an Instructional Designer may be:

   "Writing Course Objectives"
   "Writing Course Storyboards"

   ┌───┐
   │   │
   │ NOTE: Writing a duty statement involves using a verb ending in "-ing" │
   │ followed by an object of the action.   │
   │   │
   └───┘

3. Identify all tasks.
   - Have SMEs or exemplary performers[7] identify preliminary tasks.
   - Interview incumbent workers.
   - Include tasks found from Extant Data Analysis and other analyses you have conducted.
   - Observe those workers who are currently performing the job.

---

[7] SMEs are used for new positions. Exemplary performers are used for positions that already exist.

- Use questionnaires, interviews, and observations.

  For example a task involved when writing objectives:

  > "The Instructional Designer must use the standard objective format."

NOTE: When writing the task statement, use an action verb and add clarification statements when necessary. Include the names of tools and forms (references). Avoid abbreviations and jargon. Be brief. The task statement must stand alone.

---

4. Identify all sub-tasks that support the identified tasks and put them in order.

NOTE: Follow the Note above for the task level statement.

---

5. Match the KSAs for the selected tasks from your Audience Analysis. You should now be able to conduct your Critical Incident Analysis.

   For example, one skill is:

   > "Include the learned capability verb."

INDICATORS FOR USING CBT

Since Task Analysis only indicates the full range of tasks involved in the skill, you would not make a final decision on the potential use of CBT until after you have conducted Subject Matter Analysis, which determines the tasks chosen for training.

RATIONALE

The results that you obtain in your Task Analysis will provide you with the information you need to conduct a Critical Incident Analysis, which will help you to make judgments on the specific elements that your training will include.

APPLICATION TOOLS

Figure 2-6-2 can be used to structure your Task Analysis. When used with a good database management computer program, the information that you collect can be worked with easily and quickly.

Figure 2-6-2
Job/Task Breakdown Form

1. Job: A collection of duties and tasks constituting the total job responsibilities.

2. Duties: Major subdivisions of the job responsibilities performed by an individual. Duties are usually stated as a general area of responsibility, with action words ending in "ing."

3. Task: A specific function or meaningful unit of work that must be performed to accomplish the overall duty. This task achieves a single objective or output.

4. Sub-task: A step, action, operation, or activity that is a logical segment of a task that advances the work.

5. KSAs: K = Knowledge, S = Skills, A = Attitude

	To be completed after objectives are written
	Number
Job	
_____	_____ Course Objective
Duty 1.0	
_____	
Task 1.1	
_____	_____ Terminal Objective
Sub-task 1.1.1	
_____	_____ Lesson Objective
Sub-task 1.1.2	
_____	_____ Lesson Objective
Sub-task 1.1.3	
_____	_____ Lesson Objective
Sub-task 1.1.4	
_____	_____ Lesson Objective
Task 1.2	
_____	_____ Terminal Objective
Sub-task 1.2.1	
_____	_____ Lesson Objective
Sub-task 1.2.2	
_____	_____ Lesson Objective
Sub-task 1.2.3	
_____	_____ Lesson Objective

Duty 2.0

Task 2.1

_____ Terminal Objective

Sub-task 2.1.1

_____ Lesson Objective

Sub-task 2.1.2

_____ Lesson Objective

Sub-task 2.1.3

_____ Lesson Objective

Task 2.2

_____ Terminal Objective

Sub-task 2.2.1

_____ Lesson Objective

Sub-task 2.2.2

_____ Lesson Objective

CHAPTER 2-7
CRITICAL INCIDENT ANALYSIS

INTRODUCTION

After you have identified all the tasks for a specific job, your next steps are to:

(1) determine the tasks that are critical to the job **and** must be trained;
(2) identify the tasks that are nice to know (**time and budget permitting**); and
(3) determine those tasks that you will **de-select** (reject) and not train.

The focus group strategy discussed in Chapter 2-1 is useful in most situations where performance can be described by expert performers.

There will be times, however, when what is considered expert performance will be difficult to describe or capture. For example, what is it that distinguishes the performance of an effective salesperson or a good manager from an average or poor one? Critical Incident Analysis is used most effectively to define performance in clearly distinguishable areas.

Critical incidents are facts, not generalizations or opinions. They are about performance that can be pinpointed as either effective or ineffective. They are not just routine steps habitually performed correctly. Rather, they are behavioral descriptions of instances of extreme cases (characterized by success or failure) in performance.

WHAT TO DO

The process of Task Analysis described in Chapter 2-6 helps to initiate many of the other types of Front-end Analyses that are required to develop effective training programs or courses. In Critical Incident Analysis, generating the tasks that must be performed by the job holder will also generate those duties and tasks that are presently performed well and also those duties and tasks that are important, but lacking.

Those duties and tasks that are performed well should be analyzed to determine how the skills are presently learned or taught. Determining this might lead to the conclusion that where performance is presently high, there is no need for training on those skills in the program under development. The conclusion might also be that the learning techniques should be replicated and included in the training. Some of the primary reasons for task rejection are:

1. Task is *seldom* performed.
2. Task is *not critical.*
3. Task is *easily learned without training.*

Tasks that show up weak areas of performance definitely should be included in the training program if they are of high priority.

How To Do It

Use focus groups, observations, direct interviews, and questionnaires (any combinations of these that you feel are necessary) to determine the critical incidents of training. Whichever technique(s) is used, the basic procedure is to review the tasks that were generated during the Task Analysis.

Critical tasks are those that the job holder must be able to complete to successfully perform the job (under typical conditions and to the standard required). And, since there are no universally accepted considerations of criticality, you will have to construct your own. You may, however, want to consider the following when you establish your norms:

- How often the task is performed. More often generally means more critical.
- The severity of the consequences for failure to perform.
- The severity of the consequences if failure to perform is not corrected.
- Any special KSAs required to perform the task. (Are they within the skill or operational level of the person who will perform the task?)

Figures 2-7-1 and 2-7-2 provide the definitions and worksheets to rate each task. Figure 2-7-3 is a summary sheet to report each task, after each person reporting completes his or her individual worksheet (Figure 2-7-2) and your team reaches consensus.

Using your established measures of criticality, you should then:

(1) review each task with a SME or exemplary performer;
(2) identify the critical aspects of each task;
(3) determine the tasks that must be trained;
(4) create a Task Hierarchy; and
(5) list all super ordinate tasks with their subordinate tasks.

Material that is omitted may fall into three categories:

(1) prerequisite skills that the learner should know before undergoing the training (these will be the focus of your Instructional Analysis);
(2) skills beyond the range of capability or permissibility[8] of the person to be trained; and
(3) skills that are presently performed at a high enough level of proficiency.

---

[8] Some labor unions have restrictions on what tasks union members can perform.

INDICATORS FOR USING CBT

Indicators exist that CBT is a solution for delivering training, if your Critical Incident Analysis reveals that:

- the information to be used involves a computer system;
- current training is failing to meet the depth students need to be able to successfully perform the skill;
- required skills are easily taught and measured by CBT;
- the skills are knowledge based;
- the skills are performance based.

You may also find that CAI is an option, whereby some of the training would be conducted on the computer and some portions by a classroom instructor.

RATIONALE

You should not write objectives for every Job, Duty, or Task that you identified in your Task Analysis only to have to find that you discard some when you select those to be trained. Critical Incident Analysis eliminates this extra work. Critical Incident Analysis forms the basis for your Objective Analysis.

APPLICATION TOOLS

The questionnaires and interview guides that you developed for use in your Needs Assessment, along with your interview notes, evaluations, and the flowcharts you developed for your Task Analysis are some Application Tools you will use for conducting a Critical Incident Analysis.

Figures 2-7-1, 2-7-2, and 2-7-3 will be helpful in establishing the criticality of your tasks.

Figure 2-7-1
Criteria for Selecting Tasks for Training

Frequency

How often is the task performed?

No. Performing

What percent of the target population is/will perform this task?

Difficulty

How difficult is it to learn this task on the job?

Criticality

How important is this task to job performance?

Codes	Definitions
N	**Non-critical** — This code identifies tasks not critical to the job.
I	**Important** — This code identifies tasks that are important in some situations but not critical.
C	**Critical** — This code identifies tasks that must be performed correctly because of their impact on the job.

Time

How long does it normally take to perform this task?

Impact

What is the probability that this task will be performed poorly or incorrectly if the performer is not formally trained?

Delay

How long after training will it be before the trainee encounters this task?

Immediacy/Assistance

Must this task be performed on-the-spot without any assistance?

Figure 2-7-2
Task Rating Form

Each task should be rated in each of the categories below:

1. **Frequency** — How often will the task be performed?

Never		Sometimes		Always
1	2	3	4	5

2. **Performing** — What percent of the target population is/will perform this task?

Few		Some		Many
0-10%	11-30%	31-70%	71-90%	91-100%

3. **Difficulty**—How difficult is it to perform the task on the job without instructional assistance?

Very Easy	Easy	Difficult	Very Difficult	Impossible
1	2	3	4	5

4. **Criticality** — How important is it for the trainee to know how to perform the task in order to meet day-to-day performance requirements?

Not Critical	Important	Critical
N	I	C

5. **Time** — How long should it take to perform this task?

less than 10 minutes	10-20 minutes	20-30 minutes	30-40 minutes	40-50 minutes
0	1	2	3	4

50-60 minutes	more than one hour	more than 3 hours	more than 6 hours	more than one day
5	6	7	8	9

6. Impact — What is the probability that the task will be performed poorly if not formally trained?

Very low	Low	Moderate	High	Very High
1	2	3	4	5

7. Delay—How long after training will it be before the trainee encounters this task?

Two weeks	One month	Three months	Six months	One year
1	2	3	4	5

8. Immediacy/Assistance — How important is it that this task be performed on the spot with not assistance?

Hardly	Somewhat	Moderate	Very	Extremely
1	2	3	4	5

NOTE: There is no "master key" to the rating scales listed above. There is no "mathematical average" or other mathematical manipulation that will provide you with a totally sound basis for making a training decision. Use the rating scales above and the priority levels below to determine critical incidents **based on customer needs and professional judgment.**

Priority 1 — Train to mastery level.

Requires thorough training. The trainee must master the task and perform the task at the level, speed, and accuracy required on the job.

Priority 2 — Train to perform.

Training may be provided. The trainee must demonstrate that he/she can perform the task, but not necessarily with the proficiency required on the job.

Priority 3 — Train if time/situation allow.

Some or all trainees may be introduced to the task if time and/or business situation allow. However, the trainee will not be expected to perform the task as a requirement for successful completion of training.

Priority 4 — Do not train.

Task will not be taught formally at all.

Figure 2-7-3
Task Inventory Form

Task No. _____

Related Job _____

_____

Related Duty _____

_____

Indicate the priority for each of the selection criteria below that were used in the determination of each criterion.

Selection Criteria (Circle those that apply)	**Frequency**	**Percent (%) Performing**	**Difficulty**	**Criticality**
	Time	**Impact**	**Delay**	**Immediacy No Assistance**

Priority _____ Date _____

Confirmed by Subject Matter Analysis: Yes____ No ____

CHAPTER 2-8
INSTRUCTIONAL ANALYSIS

INTRODUCTION

You've assessed and analyzed the job from a number of perspectives and you have sufficient data to support the training needs. But there is still information that is missing, even though your Audience Analysis was well done. You need to get behind the major outcomes for your training design and examine the prerequisite skills that must be mastered for a student to achieve the goals of your training. Instructional Analysis is the tool that will help you to identify both the upper limits of your training goals as well as the prerequisite knowledge and skills that your learners are already presumed to know.

WHAT TO DO

Much has been written (Seels & Glasgow, 1990; Dick & Carey, 1990; Gagné, Briggs, & Wager, 1988) to help you through this Analysis Phase. In keeping with our how-to approach, we have selected two important skill areas covered by Instructional Analysis to focus this chapter on. These are:

(1) prerequisite job skills; and
(2) language skills.

Analyzing the skill levels your students possess going into training will help you design CBT that is both appropriate and effective. Lists of prerequisite skills are also important for you because, while job descriptions will set the upper limits of training, prerequisite skills set the lower limits. Entry level skills that the job holders are presumed to know do not have to be trained.

Ensuring that readability levels are correct and that your students understand the language of instruction are important to ensure that learning will take place.

HOW TO DO IT

Keep a record of any additional information on audience motivation and background that you feel may be helpful to you in designing materials that meet the personal as well as practical needs of your audience. Examples of this information might be:

(1) experience with CBT;
(2) learning preferences (team; individual);
(3) language ability or preference;
(4) previous training or job experience;
(5) group composition (homogenous or heterogeneous); and
(6) special requirements (wheelchair access, signing, etc.).

Sorting out your information and comparing it to the tasks that have been selected for training will help you to determine the prerequisite job skills (item 4 above) that your audience already possesses and will tell you what tasks they can perform. This information will help you to eliminate these tasks from your training as you begin setting training objectives and constructing preliminary designs (items 1, 2, 5, and 6 above).

Analyzing language skills (item 3 above) requires a two-stage approach. Stage one requires that you find out your audience's language ability and preference. This can be done in interviews or on questionnaires. Once a language of instruction is selected, Stage two is to ensure that it is used consistently with different audience reading ability levels. An effective method we have used (for English) is the Fog Index, one of many readability scales that are available. The method for calculating readability using the Fog Index is shown in Figure 2-8-1.

INDICATORS FOR USING CBT

CBT is a solution for training if your Instructional Analysis reveals that training must be individualized because students are highly diverse in:

- the amount of information that they know about the subject;
- their cultural backgrounds;
- their language background;
- their experience on the job;
- their preferred methods of learning;
- special accessibility requirements under disability laws and regulations; and
- special considerations regarding equal opportunity.

RATIONALE

Taking the time to analyze prerequisite job skills and confirming language levels and ability will ensure that your training program will be as effective as it will be understandable.

APPLICATION TOOLS

Several word processing computer programs and grammar checkers have readability "checkers" built into them. If you have one of these built-in readability "checkers," use it. If not, we have provided an explanation of how to manually compute the Fog Index in Figure 2-8-1.

Figure 2-8-1
Calculating The Fog Index

The Fog Index, developed by Robert Gunning, expresses readability as the number of years of schooling required to read the text with ease. Follow these steps to check readability:

1. Select a representative (2-3 pages) sample of text.

2. Count the number of words it contains.

3. Count the number of sentences it contains.

4. Count the number of difficult words. Difficult words are those defined as having three or more syllables and/or ending with "ly" or "ing." Exceptions to this are:

    *   Capitalized words.

    *   Combinations of short, easy words like task-scheduler, machine-foreman, etc.

    *   Verb forms made into three syllables by adding "ed" or "es" like adjusted, inserted, assesses.

5. Determine the average sentence length. Divide the number of words by the number of sentences.

6. Determine the percentage of difficult words in the sample:

$$\% \text{ of difficult words} = \frac{\text{number of difficult words x 1000}}{\text{number of words}}$$

7. Use the following formula to calculate the Fog Index:

    Fog Index = Average Sentence Length + % of difficult words **x 0.4**

8. Repeat the process using two or three random samples from the beginning, middle, and end of the course materials, or from different authors, to see if there is uniformity.

CHAPTER 2-9
SUBJECT MATTER ANALYSIS

INTRODUCTION

You have almost completed the Analysis Phase. Before you move to the Design Phase you must conduct Subject Matter Analysis to identify the specific content your training will contain for the audience and tasks you have identified.

WHAT TO DO

A well structured Subject Matter Analysis should examine the results of all your analyses and all relevant documentation. For each job you analyze, you should obtain at least one, preferably more, exemplary performer who will identify specific job success or failure factors. These exemplary performers become your SMEs. You need to provide guidelines for these exemplary performers before they review the subject matter.

HOW TO DO IT

Follow these steps in conducting a Subject Matter Analysis:

1. Identify and obtain time commitment from your exemplary performers. They are people who:
    *   currently perform the job correctly;
    *   are recognized by the organization as knowledgeable in the tasks to be trained; and
    *   can identify performance success and failure.
2. Have the exemplary performers review the results of your analyses and other documentation. This step may also be conducted in a review panel format.
3. Provide your reviewers with guidelines for reviewing the subject matter. Some guidelines to consider are:
    *   comments should be as objective as possible;
    *   constructive criticism is encouraged;
    *   provide examples of desired performance;
    *   provide examples of desired changes; and
    *   use technical terminology as descriptors when appropriate.

The main question that Subject Matter Analysis must answer is: "Do these tasks and the order that they are listed in accurately reflect the totality of successful job performance?"

Once your exemplary performers validate the hierarchy, they should provide the steps for performing each duty and task. This becomes the Content Outline for your Design Phase, where the tasks listed under each duty become the lesson designs.

INDICATORS FOR USING CBT

Indicators exist that CBT is a solution for delivering the training if:

- The material can be presented at the appropriate level through a computer.
- Students can see skills adequately demonstrated via a computer presentation.
- Students can interact with the computer at the appropriate level.

RATIONALE

The results of the Subject Matter Analysis supply the content for instruction. Accuracy, emphasis, and timeliness are detailed and examples that can be used in training are verified.

APPLICATION TOOLS

The lists, charts, and forms that you used in your Front-end Analysis, along with your interview notes and evaluations, are the Application Tools you use for conducting a Subject Matter Analysis. These all roll up into an Analysis Report, which is generated using summaries of data that you have been collecting using a flexible database management program. An Analysis Report outline is shown in Figure 2-9-1.

Figure 2-9-1
Analysis Report*

1. Introduction
(A brief description of the purpose of this report)

2. Description of the job analyzed.
(Audience Analysis)

3. Description of the job performer's needs.
(Instructional Analysis)

4. Task Hierarchy.
(Task Analysis/Subject Matter Analysis/Critical Incident Analysis)

5. Objectives.
(Objective Analysis)

6. Sources of additional information.
(Extant Data Analysis)

7. Attachments:
Rejected Tasks *(Critical Incident Analysis)*

* A description of the section content or the source of it follows each heading in parentheses.

CHAPTER 2-10
OBJECTIVE ANALYSIS

INTRODUCTION

Now you are ready to write the objectives for the CBT course based on the results of your Critical Incident Analysis. Writing clear objectives is probably the second most critical element to developing effective instruction — right after conducting a thorough Assessment/Analysis of what is needed. However, writing clear objectives that effectively communicate the instructional intent is little understood, and seldom done, even though nearly all pay homage to the principle that good instruction follows good objectives. Thus, we are devoting a considerable portion of this handbook to this topic — indicative of the importance we attach to it.

Confusion still remains about writing and using objectives. And everyone who adds a unique twist usually adds to the confusion. After all the years professionals have had to straighten out terminology, designers still don't know whose objective to use, or when.

The answer is an approach that allows teams to eliminate the confusion and get past this stumbling block and on to producing the course. The "process approach" outlined in this chapter can eliminate the confusion about objectives and still stay within the existing body of knowledge about objectives and use the same terminology.

Projects where teams have used this process have produced clear objectives that effectively communicate the content to everyone.

WHAT TO DO

You now use the numbering system from the form in Figure 2-6-2 and the results of Figures 2-7-3 and 2-9-1 to turn the tasks into objectives.

Objective Hierarchy

Write objectives in this order:

1. Course Objective   Concisely states the goal for the entire course in one or two sentences, clearly indicating what the students should know (skills) or be able to do (performance) after completing the entire course.

2.	Performance Objectives	These objectives never actually go into the course. They are written for instructional designers to communicate with each other. These are the five part objectives that eventually make up the Terminal and Lesson Objectives as explained in the Process Approach described in this chapter.
3.	Terminal Objectives	State the terminal knowledge, performance, and attitudes that a student will demonstrate at the end of a unit of instruction; the knowledge and performance that the student will demonstrate in order to achieve the Course Objective.
4.	Lesson Objectives	The specific knowledge, performance, or attitudes that the student will demonstrate at the end of a lesson. Each lesson will have at least one Terminal Objective but, depending on clustering of the content, a lesson may contain more than one Terminal Objective.

NOTE: Be sure you complete the Job/Task Breakdown Form (Figure 2-6-2) after writing and renumbering the terminal and lesson objectives.

The emphasis is on "team" because objectives written by one person, within, adjunct to, or disassociated from the team are not as effective in overall course development. The benefits of using a process approach to writing objectives are that:

1. For the first time you know at the beginning of the task, how to write objectives.
2. At the end of the activity, everyone involved understands the content of the course and where the parts assigned to them fit into the larger scheme. As with any team activity, each member must leave ego at the door and be willing to engage in the give-and-take that this process of writing objectives requires.

You have theoretically completed the Objective Hierarchy when you finalize the objectives. However, even into the Design Phase you many find that some content does not work where you thought it would now that the full content of the task is evolving. You can still move objectives and the accompanying content throughout the Design Phase.

The Basis of the Process

Of all that is written on objectives, Mager provided the basics in his 1962 book, *Preparing Instructional Objectives*. Gagné, Briggs, and Wager in *Principles of Instructional Design* (1988) have, in our opinion, improved on these basics better than anyone.

Domains of Learning

There are five domains in which learning occurs (Gagné, Briggs, & Wager, 1988). These domains form the basis for writing objectives. The designer must first identify whether the training content that will be developed deals with the KSAs. Course development teams often forget that they are training more than intellectual skills, especially in the field of technical training. Although Gagné and associates include motor skills and attitudes among their learned capabilities, there is a need for a more complete understanding of all the learning domains. The five domains are:

1.	Cognitive	Dealing with the thought processes.
2.	Affective	Dealing with feelings and attitudes.
3.	Motor	Dealing with the learning of actual physical movements.
4.	Psychomotor	Dealing with cognitive thought processes involved in physical movements that have been brought to the automatic level (can do them without thinking).
5.	Metacognitive	Dealing with the cognitive thought processes involved in "learning how to learn" that have been brought to the automatic level (strategies for approaching learning tasks that one uses without thinking about them).

Levels of Intellectual Skills Within Cognitive Domain

Gagné, Briggs, and Wager present the best outline of the various levels of intellectual skills required for learning within the Cognitive Domain. The seven levels are:

1.	Discriminations	Being able to see, hear, or feel the differences between incoming stimulus situations.
2.	Concrete Concept	Being able to identify one or more instances of a class of items.
3.	Defined Concept	Being able to classify objects or events according to certain attributes and functions.
4.	Rule	Being able to form classifications that distinguish relationships between and among concepts (concrete or defined).
5.	Problem-solving	Being able to apply rules to new situations.
6.	Cognitive Strategies	Being able to apply problem-solving strategies when approaching a learning situation.
7.	Verbal Information	Being able to repeat verbal information with comprehension of what is verbalized.

Levels Within Affective Domain

Krathwohl edited *A Taxonomy of Educational Objectives II* in 1964, which outlined levels within the Affective Domain. Krathwohl listed five levels but the first two, Receiving and Responding, have been combined here because receiving cannot be measured unless the student responds. The four levels are:

1.	Receiving and Responding	Verbally stating the learner is sensitive to or has adopted a value or attitude.
2.	Valuing	Demonstrating by behaviors and actions that one is sensitive to or has adopted a value or attitude.
3.	Organization	Making comparisons, theorizing, organizing, balancing, defining, and formulating criteria to evaluate behaviors, codes of conduct, and standards for values determination.
4.	Characterization	Changing behavior as a result of reorganization and establishing consistent, increasingly more mature, behavior patterns.

Levels Within Motor/Psychomotor

Harrow (1972) published a taxonomy of levels of functioning within the Psychomotor Domain. Three are listed here as examples. We will only deal with those most relevant to training. The remaining levels are eliminated for the sake of not further complicating the issue at hand. This is not to leave the impression that these levels are unimportant. Refer to Harrow's book, *A Taxonomy in the Psychomotor Domain,* for a complete discussion of all of the levels. The three presented here are representative of the levels that are most commonly used in course development for business and industry.

Here is an important distinction. Motor objectives are those that emphasize actually teaching the motor skill. Psychomotor objectives have as their basis the intellectual knowledge and skills that underlie the motor activity. Psychomotor skills are motor skills that have been brought to the automatic level through learning that integrates them with cognitive processes.

LEVELS WITHIN MOTOR

1.	Reflex Movements	Voluntary or involuntary physical movements or actions.
2.	Basic Fundamental Movements	More coordinated reflex movements such as reaching, grasping, crawling, manipulating physical objects, walking.

LEVELS WITHIN PSYCHOMOTOR

1.	Perceptual	distinguishing between the self and surroundings: (a) *Kinesthetic Discriminations* — the relation of one's body to surrounding objects and controlling one's body in relation to the surrounding space.

(b) *Auditory Discrimination* — the ability of the learner to differentiate among various sounds; their pitch, intensity, directionality, and to reproduce the sound if necessary.

(c) *Visual Discrimination* — distinguish between form and details of objects; the ability to visually track an object; the ability to remember the attributes of an object; select the dominant figure from the background; ability to recognize the consistency of shapes and forms.

(d) *Tactile Discrimination* — the ability to differentiate between the textures or form of objects through the sense of touch.

(e) *Coordinated Abilities* — the coordination of two or more of the above perceptual capabilities.

Metacognitive Strategies

Metacognition is the integration of the cognitive, affective, motor, and psychomotor domains. It involves the internal strategies one employs when approaching a task or in solving a problem — learning how to learn. Metacognition is probably the least written about and least understood — but the most important — learning domain because it integrates all of the other domains.

Superior training should go beyond simply providing the knowledge and skills necessary for a task. Teaching processes and problem-solving strategies that students can generalize to other situations are the highest levels of instruction that can be provided.

The best learners develop these strategies on their own. However, this should not be left to chance. There are discernible, discrete steps to teaching metacognitive strategies to those who do not have them or for instilling in students a desired or efficient method of attacking a problem.

Some of the best information on teaching metacognitive strategies comes from the work of Gordon Alley and Donald Deshler (1979) with learning-handicapped adolescents. However, the same principles that they teach to educationally challenged individuals are those that others learn on their own. Their analysis of the metacognitive process is excellent and is based soundly in the body of theory about the ways that people learn effectively and efficiently. The eight steps in learning a metacognitive strategy are:

1. Have the student perform the targeted task or skill to observe how he or she approaches the task.

2. Point out to the student precisely the way that he or she approaches the task.
3. Explain to the student the new way that he or she will be taught to approach the task (derived from Task Analysis).
4. Demonstrate the new approach to the student, carefully pointing out the advantages of the new one over the old one the student was using.
5. The student should be encouraged to ask questions at any time during the demonstration.
6. The student must verbally rehearse the steps in the process until he or she can state them without error and fluidly. (Alley and Deshler refer to this as "rehearsal to the automatic level.")
7. Practice using the new strategy on controlled materials that do not have any other elements (such as a very high reading level, complex chapter structure, or large numbers that must be calculated).
8. Practice with actual materials that the student will have to use to complete the task in order for him or her to transfer the strategy to the workplace and generalize it to other situations.

Gagné's learned capabilities of problem-solving and cognitive strategies begin to reach the metacognitive level because there are components of both capabilities in metacognition. However, these two learned capabilities must be carried to levels beyond teaching a problem-solving or cognitive strategy to methods for recognizing similarities between situations and applying generalized rules to reach a solution.

How To Do It

Writing Objectives Within the Domains of Learning
There are many proponents of what are commonly known as "objectives" and each proponent has his/her own idea about what should be included in the elements of an objective.

Performance Objectives
Gagné, Briggs, and Wager present the "Performance Objective," which contains five elements:

1.	Situation	The stimulus situation, the given, or under what circumstances the behavior will be observed.
2.	Learned Capability	The type of learning outcome the demonstrated behavior represents strictly defined by certain verbs for each level of intellectual skill. You cannot use these words as the Action Verb in an objective. Table 2-10-1 lists these verbs and explains their meanings as learned capabilities.
3.	Object	The content of the learner's performance.
4.	Action Verb	How the performance will be completed.

5. Tools, Constraints, and Conditions

The special tools needed, the constraints to, or the actual conditions under which the performance will be observed.

Table 2-10-1
Gagné, Briggs, and Wager's Learned Capabilities and Accompanying Verbs for Developing Performance Objectives

Learned Capability	Capability Verb
Discrimination	Discriminates
Concrete Concept	Identifies
Defined Concept	Classifies
Rule	Demonstrates
Problem-solving	Generates
Cognitive Strategy	Adopts
Verbal Information	States
Motor Skill*	Executes
Attitude*	Chooses

* Note that the capabilities and verbs have been included here for the Psychomotor Domain (Motor Skill) and the Affective Domain (Attitude). Gagné *et al.* include these two domains under intellectual skills.

Terminal Objectives

Mager's objective is identical to those of Gagné and associates with the exception that the learned capability verb is removed. Mager proposes a four-step objective ("who is performing" is always understood by all writers of objectives to be "the student"). Table 2-10-2 compares these differences.

Table 2-10-2
Types of Objectives

Objective Hierarchy	Purpose	Author
Performance Objectives	Communication between Instructional Designers.	Gagné, Briggs, & Wager
Terminal Objectives	Identify the observable performance that the learner will possess at the end of the lesson.	Mager
Lesson Objectives*	Specify what learning will occur, and in what sequence, leading the learner to achieve the Terminal Objective.	Mager
Goals	General task statements that describe the intended outcome of the learning.	Mager

* Mager calls these Enabling Objectives.

Lesson Objectives

The Lesson Objectives are the objectives that identify the specific way the learner will demonstrate that he or she has achieved the Terminal Objective.

Model for Developing Objectives

Another problem is that most authors take the easiest way out when they begin to provide examples of objectives at each of the domains and levels. If you work in the field of training development, you find little use in an example of a psychomotor objective involving learning to ride a bicycle. The following examples will use adult learning situations in both the technical and soft skills training environment and model how to write objectives in each domain and at each level.

A list of verbs to use when translating Performance Objectives into Terminal Objectives is found in Appendix A. The list is especially suited to objectives to be achieved via CBT.

Objectives for Technical Skills

Training in technical skills usually involves developing training for a piece of equipment or machinery. The example used to model writing objectives in the manufacturing environment involves the maintenance of a piece of electronic equipment. Each objective is identified by the domain and the level.

Cognitive/Discrimination

Given a diagram of the electronic instrument **(situation)**, the student will discriminate **(learned capability)** each functional part by circling **(action verb)** each major part **(object)** with complete accuracy **(special conditions)**.

Cognitive/Concrete Concept

Given an operational model of the electronic instrument **(situation)**, the student will identify **(learned capability)** the various alignment and adjustment procedures **(object)** by verbalizing **(action verb)** the procedure for each different type with complete accuracy **(special conditions)**.

Cognitive/Defined Concept

Given the term for a major part of the electronic instrument **(situation)**, the student will classify **(learned capability)** the sub-assemblies of that part **(object)** by writing **(action verb)** the parts beside the term with complete accuracy **(special conditions)**.

Cognitive/Rule

Given a defined problem in a major part of the electronic instrument (**situation**), the student will demonstrate (**learned capability**) knowledge of trouble-shooting procedures (**object**) by verbalizing (**action verb**) the trouble-shooting procedure with complete accuracy (**special condition**).

Cognitive/Problem-Solving

Given an actual problem in a major part of the electronic instrument (**situation**), the student generates (**learned capability**) a method to repair the problem (**object**) by verbally eliminating (**action verb**) the possible reasons for the problem and the primary cause of the problem (**constraint**).

Cognitive/Cognitive Strategy

Given an unidentified problem in the electronic instrument (**situation**), the student adopts (**learned capability**) a strategy of listing (**action verb**) the available information (**object**) that will locate the primary problem (**special condition**).

Cognitive/Verbal Information

Given a maintenance handbook for the electronic instrument (**situation**), the student will state (**learned capability**) the diagnostic procedure for repairing the instrument by reading a section on diagnostics (**object**) and verbally summarizing (**action verb**) the procedural steps in the correct sequence and correct number of steps (**condition**).

Affective/Receiving and Responding

Given a problem that might occur with the electronic instrument (**situation**), the student chooses (**learned capability**) to begin explaining the procedure for repairing the instrument (**object**) by verbalizing (**action verb**) the emergency shut down safety procedures before stating the repair procedure (**constraint**), thus showing concern for safety procedures.

Affective/Valuing

Given an identified problem with the electronic instrument (**situation**), the student chooses (**learned capability**) to perform (**action verb**) the emergency shut down safety procedures (**object**) before beginning to repair the problem (**constraint**).

Affective/Organization

Given a problem with the electronic instrument and the choice to follow or ignore safety procedures (**situation**), the student chooses (**learned capability**) to verbalize (**action verb**) to another student the pros and cons of working on the instrument without following safety procedures (**object**) before beginning to work on the problem (**constraint**), thus showing concern for safety.

Affective/Characterization

Given a problem with the electronic instrument and without realizing that the student is being observed (**situation**), the student will choose (**learned capability**) to follow the safety procedures (**object**) by completing (**action verb**) the safety shut down procedure in every situation (**constraint**).

Motor/Reflex

None.

Motor/Basic Fundamental Movements

Given an identified problem in the electrical distribution system of the electronic instrument (**situation**), the student will execute (**learned capability**) attaching (**action verb**) the volt meter to the ground and appropriate resistor or lead point (**object**) to the terminals (**constraints/tools**).

Psychomotor/Perceptual — Visual Discrimination

Given an identified problem in the electrical distribution system of the electronic instrument (**situation**), the student will execute (**learned capability**) the diagnostic procedures by correctly attaching (**action verb**) the volt meter to the ground and appropriate resistor or lead point (**object**) with the correct ends on the correct terminals (**constraint/tools**).

Metacognitive

Given an unidentified problem in an electronic instrument's electrical system but without identifying a specific instrument (**situation**), develops (e.g., adopts) (**learned capability**) a strategy for approaching the situation (**object**) by listing (**action verb**) the steps necessary to approach the problem without prior instruction (**constraint**).

Objectives for Soft Skills

Soft skills training is training in those intangibles such as delivering service, management techniques, and interpersonal skills.[9] The example used here to demonstrate how the objective-writing process is adapted to soft skills is supervisory leadership skills.

Cognitive/Discrimination

Given a problem scenario involving one or more group members (**situation**), discriminates (**learned capability**) between the needs of the individual versus the needs of the work group (**object**) by responding (**action verb**) appropriately (**condition**) to both.

---

[9] Generally known as management skills.

Cognitive/Concrete Concept

Given a selected work unit (**situation**), identifies (**learned capability**) internal and external customers (**object**) by verbally listing (**action verb**) all (**condition**) characteristics.

Cognitive/Defined Concept

Given a list of behaviors (**situation**), classifies (**learned capability**) those behaviors as acceptable or unacceptable (**object**) by listing (**action verb**) them in two columns with complete accuracy (**condition**).

Cognitive/Rule

In the workplace (**situation**), demonstrates (**learned capability**) vision and direction for continuous improvement (**object**) by developing and sharing (**action verb**) a vision statement designed to gain work group members' understanding of, and commitment to, continuous improvement (**conditions**).

Cognitive/Problem-Solving

To ensure that work group members have the information, training, responsibility, and resources to accomplish their assignments (**situation**), generates (**learned capability**) strategies for analyzing, monitoring and aligning (**action verb**) routine elements (**object**) of work group performance with customer requirements and quality standards (**conditions**).

Cognitive/Cognitive Strategy

Given related needs to achieve objectives and to empower others (**situation**), adopts (**learned capability**) a strategy of responding directly and positively to others (**object**) by providing (**action verb**) accurate and timely information (**conditions**).

Cognitive/Verbal Information

Given a list of quality standards (**situation**), states (**learned capability**), verbally (**action verb**), the information, training, and resources needed by the work group to achieve those standards (**object**) with complete accuracy (**conditions**).

Affective/ Receiving and Responding

Given the continuous improvement philosophy and a sample work situation (**situation**), chooses (**learned capability**) to speak (**action verb**) in such a way (object) that shows support for the philosophy (**conditions**).

Affective/Valuing

Given a representative workplace situation **(situation)**, chooses **(learned capability)** to support company values **(object)** by consciously acting **(action verb)** in ways that are perceived to be consistent with these values **(constraints)**.

Affective/Organization

Given a workplace situation where quality standards could be ignored **(situation)**, chooses **(learned capability)** to relate **(action verb)** the benefits of following quality standards **(object)** to the individual and the organization using words that adhere to company philosophy **(conditions)**.

Affective/Characterization

After individual counseling from a superior regarding an employees' actions **(situation)**, chooses **(learned capability)** to change his or her behavior **(object)** by acting **(action verb)** in ways that demonstrate company philosophy **(condition)**.

Motor/Reflex

None.

Motor/Basic Fundamental Movements

None.

Psychomotor/Perceptual Kinesthetic Discrimination

Given a work environment **(situation)**, executes **(learned capability)** changes **(action verb)** that conform to ergonomics **(object)** in the opinion of the employees in that environment **(conditions)**.

Metacognitive

Given an unidentified problem in the work environment **(situation)**, develops (e.g., adopts) **(learned capability)** a strategy for approaching the problem **(object)** by listing **(action verb)** the steps necessary to approach the problem without prior instruction **(constraint)**.

Terminal and Lesson Objectives from Performance Objectives

Once the Performance Objectives are agreed upon by the designers, three additional steps in the design process have been completed:

1. Designers have a clear understanding of the intended level of the training.
2. Terminal Objectives have concurrently been developed.
3. Lesson Objectives have concurrently been developed.

So, even if you think that developing Performance Objectives is too time consuming, it really isn't, if you consider all of the other tasks that are completed with this one activity.

But how were these last two tasks completed simply by writing Performance Objectives? Within the Performance Objective exists the Terminal Objective and the Lesson Objective. For example, let's use the first objective written for the manufacturing course:

Cognitive/Discrimination
> Given a diagram of the electronic instrument **(situation)**, the student will discriminate each functional part **(learned capability)** by circling **(action verb)** each major part **(object)** with complete accuracy **(special conditions)**.

As the model prescribes, the Terminal Objective is derived by taking out the action verb and the special conditions. Here is the result:

Terminal Objective
> Given a diagram of the electronic instrument, the student will *discriminate* each functional part.

To form the Lesson Objective, remove the learned capability verb from the Performance Objective. The resulting objective is:

Lesson Objective
> Given a diagram of the electronic instrument, the student will *circle* all major parts with complete accuracy.

The resulting Terminal and Lesson Objectives fit the definitions found in Table 2-10-2:

> Terminal Objective — List the observable performance that the learner will possess at the end of the lesson.

> Lesson Objectives — Identify what learning will occur, and in what sequence, leading the learner to achieve the Terminal Objective.

Writing Tests That Match Objectives

Developing tests and/or other performance measures are the outgrowth of objectives. After you write the course and lesson objectives, you should then go to Chapter 3-8 and write your tests. Your job of test writing is much easier as a result of having used this process of writing objectives because you know what the terminal objective of each lesson is and the verb in each objective tells you how to measure the objective (knowledge or performance, etc.). The way that the objective will be measured lies in the Lesson Objective. You can also use the objectives as a guide to determine the level that the lesson must be written to in order to adequately measure the test item. A lesson with an objective that states that a student will be able to solve problems cannot teach only to the level of making discriminations.

For example, in the sample objectives above, the Terminal Objective of the lesson is to have the student "... *discriminate* each functional part of the electronic instrument." The way the objective will be measured is in the Lesson Objective: "... the student will *circle* all major parts with complete accuracy." This lesson should provide information that will allow the student to make the appropriate discriminations. The lesson need not teach the student how to circle the major parts because there is no motor or psychomotor objective that requires that skill to be taught. The skill of being physically able to draw and perceptually discriminating a circle is a prerequisite skill — one that doesn't need to be taught in the course presently under development. The true measure is that, in the end, the correct answers are circled.

INDICATORS FOR USING CBT

Your medium of delivery should be determined before you write objectives. If the medium is CBT, you need to write your objectives using the verb lists in Appendix A so that the outcomes you desire can be measured by CBT.

RATIONALE

The result of using this process for writing objectives is that the team will thoroughly understand the intent of the final objectives and congeal the ID's concept of the training. A goal statement can be developed into an instructional design objective that is a defined concept rather than a cognitive strategy or a rule instead of problem-solving. Eliminating that basic variance is what results in the designers having a greater understanding of what the course actually intends to teach, and at what level of the various domains.

APPLICATION TOOLS

The Terminal Objective Verb List in Appendix A should guide you to using the correct verb for your terminal objectives at the appropriate level of training. We are providing this list with definitions so that you can choose verbs to write objectives that can be precisely measured by CBT. Precision is critical when you write test items that match your objectives.

Use a form similar to Figure 2-10-1 for the layout of the objectives. Use a separate form for each TO and its associated LO. Once all objectives are written and numbered, go back to the Figure 2-6-2 and write the number of the objective on the right side of the form next to the Job, Duty, and Task number that corresponds to each objective. This becomes your cross reference matrix in your Analysis Report (Chapter 2-9).

Figure 2-10-1
Objectives Form

Course _____ Unit _____

Lesson _____ Author _____

TERMINAL OBJECTIVE
Number

LESSON OBJECTIVE
Number

Unit 2 References

These are specific references for the chapters in this unit. For additional resources on topics in this unit, see the Bibliography.

Chapter 2-1

Gagné, R., Briggs, L., & Wager, W. (1988). *Principles of Instructional Design.* Third Edition. New York: Holt, Rinehart, & Winston.

Lee, W. (1993). The Parable of Concurrent Development. *Performance & Instruction,* 32 (8), pp. 12-13.

Lee, W. & Roadman, K. (1991). Linking Needs Assessment to Performance Based Evaluation. *Performance & Instruction,* 30 (6), pp. 4-6.

Seels, B. & Glasgow, Z. (1990). *Exercises in Instructional Design.* Columbus, OH: Merrill Publishing Company.

Shrock, S. & Coscarelli, W. (1989). *Criterion Referenced Test Development.* Reading, MA: Addison-Wesley Publishing Company.

Chapter 2-2

Dick, W. & Carey, L. (1990). *The Systematic Design of Instruction.* Third Edition. Glenview, IL: Scott, Foresman.

Gilbert, T. (1978). *Human Competence.* New York: McGraw-Hill.

Kaufman, R. (1994). *A Needs Assessment Audit. Performance and Instruction,* 33 (2), pp. 14-16.

Miller, A. & Irving, (1989). Pragmatic Approach to Evaluation of Interactive Media Training Programs. *Thirtieth ADCIS Conference Proceedings.* Philadelphia, PA, pp. 194-199.

Chapter 2-3

Dick, W. & Carey, L. (1990). *The Systematic Design of Instruction.* Third Edition. Glenview, IL: Scott, Foresman.

Chapter 2-4

Dick, W. & Carey, L. (1990). *The Systematic Design of Instruction.* Third Edition. Glenview, IL: Scott, Foresman.

Chapter 2-5

Dick, W. & Carey, L. (1990). *The Systematic Design of Instruction.* Third Edition. Glenview, IL: Scott, Foresman.

Chapter 2-6

Dick, W. & Carey, L. (1990). *The Systematic Design of Instruction.* Third Edition. Glenview, IL: Scott, Foresman.

Chapter 2-7

Briggs, L., Editor. (1977). *Instructional Design.* Englewood Cliffs, NJ: Educational Technology Publications.

Dick, W. & Carey, L. (1990). *The Systematic Design of Instruction.* Third Edition. Glenview, IL: Scott, Foresman.

Seels, B. & Glasgow, Z. (1990). *Exercises in Instructional Design.* Columbus, OH: Merrill Publishing Company.

Chapter 2-8

Dick, W. & Carey, L. (1990). *The Systematic Design of Instruction.* Third Edition. Glenview, IL: Scott, Foresman.

Gagné, R., Briggs, L., & Wager, W. (1988). *Principles of Instructional Design.* Third Edition. New York: Holt, Rinehart, & Winston.

Gunning, Robert. (1968). *The Technique of Clear Writing.* New York: McGraw-Hill.

Seels, B. & Glasgow, Z. (1990). *Exercises in Instructional Design.* Columbus, OH: Merrill Publishing Company.

Chapter 2-9

Dick, W. & Carey, L. (1990). *The Systematic Design of Instruction.* Third Edition. Glenview, IL: Scott, Foresman.

Chapter 2-10

Alley, G. & Deshler, D. (1979). *Teaching the Learning Disabled Adolescent: Strategies and Methods.* Denver: Love Publishing Company.

Gagné, R., Briggs, L., & Wager, W. (1988). *Principles of Instructional Design*. Third Edition. New York: Holt, Rinehart, & Winston.

Harrow, A. Ed. (1972). *A Taxonomy of the Psychomotor Domain*. New York: David McKay.

Krathwohl, D., Ed. (1964). *Taxonomy of Educational Objectives: Handbook II*. New York: David McKay.

Mager, R. (1962). *Preparing Instructional Objectives*. Palo Alto, CA: Fearon Publishers.

UNIT 3

Design

A project team meets to determine the Course Design Specifications for the CBT course.

INTRODUCTION

The Assessment and Analysis Phase is over. You have before you your objectives and the task hierarchy that tells you what tasks should be trained. The content of the tasks to be trained are in the order they should be presented based on the Subject Matter Analysis.

Now you enter the Design Phase. In this phase you will:
- develop Course Design and Development Specifications;
- write Unit and Lesson Outlines; and
- develop a Detailed Course Outline.

You need to complete the following tasks to achieve the goals of the Design Phase. Each task will be covered in a chapter of this Unit. At the end of this Unit you will have a complete Course Outline.

UNIT **C**ONTENT

This unit will discuss the following topics related to the design of CBT:

1. **Writing Specifications**
   General Presentation Style
   Text
   Grammar
   Editing Symbols
2. **Information Structure**
   Concepts
   Processes
   Procedures
   Principles
   Facts
3. **Lesson Structure**
   Instructional Events
4. **Course Outline**
   Flowcharts
   Components of a Unit Outline
   Components of a Lesson Outline
   Components of a Detailed Course Outline
5. **Designing the User Interface**
   Screen Layout
   Student Control
   Interactivity
6. **Storyboarding and Review Cycles**
   Storyboard Format
   Types of Reviews
7. **Audio and Video**
   Development Time/Cost
   Calling for Video and Audio
8. **Questions, Tests, and Feedback**
   Types of Tests
      Advantages
      Disadvantages
   Types of Questions
      Constructing Valid Questions
   Placement of Questions
      Embedded
      Quiz
      Test

CHAPTER 3-1
WRITING SPECIFICATIONS

INTRODUCTION

Writing Specifications describe the general presentation style, text, grammar, and editing symbols that you must establish to govern the design and development of lesson specifications, storyboards, student guides, and other training materials. These elements affect the look and the feel of the final product at the end of the Development Phase and describe how to get there.

All Course Design Specifications (CDS)governing the production of CBT should come *from* the work group that will be implementing them; specifications should never be *imposed by* another group. Those specifications that deal with writing as well as all other aspects of courseware design are discussed in subsequent chapters of this unit. The course design and production team should hold meetings internally and with the customer to determine these specifications. After these specifications are completed, your team and the customer should sign off on the specification document. Then the specifications should be handed to the team that will use them when they review materials and CBT lessons.

Everyone needs to understand that the specifications are the beginning point of the project. Don't set them in cement. You may find that once you begin implementing the specifications, some things that you thought would work well don't produce the desired results.

The disparity between early ideas and later application is probably the best reason why your entire team should work together to develop a prototype design to determine which specifications work and which don't, as well as which are difficult to implement but you don't want to change them because they represent good design.

If designers go off on their own and begin creating a design, they might come across a good idea but it might be too far into the Design Phase to make it practical to go back and change all other materials affected by the change. A prototype gets everyone involved, gives everyone the chance to give their input, increases the chances of the specifications being used because all team members "buy-in" to them, and prevents having good ideas being overcome by events.

WHAT TO DO

Use standard writing style guides to borrow the best aspects of style and format that fit your particular needs. The important thing is to establish standards that everyone can follow. There are many accepted writing styles and the preference of the customer should be your guiding factor. Writing specifications must address:

- general lesson presentation style and format;
- text and grammatical standards; and
- use and understanding of editing symbols.

How To Do It

While we can't give you a definitive set of Course Design Specifications here (many rely on preferences regarding style and format), there are some general principles that you should be aware of when developing your own set of specifications.

General Presentation Style

1. Keep the presentation of the content concise.
2. Keep the tone positive but don't be too personal in the wording of text or audio.

   For example:

   Appropriate: "Your answer is correct. Continue to the next exercise."
   Inappropriate: "WOW! Your answer was great! See if you can do that well on all of the exercises."
3. Always provide immediate feedback for students.
4. Always use statements to make transitions; never use a question (i.e., embedded question).

   For example:

   > "In the last section of this lesson you learned about the characteristics of a careful listener. In this section you will see a demonstration of how careful listening can avoid a negative situation with a co-worker."
5. Purpose of special effects (also known as "bells and whistles") should be to draw attention to important concepts — not to demonstrate the computer's capabilities. Animation is effective to show the flow of a concept or process. Any special capability used to excess actually detracts from learning.
6. Use build screens[10] to present information to students a piece at a time.
7. Always provide examples of the correct way to do something. Use non-examples sparingly (i.e., when you want to emphasize common errors). Students may inadvertently learn the incorrect method rather than the correct method by showing non-examples.
8. Don't use stereotypical roles, e.g., for females or minorities. For example, don't have women always perform secretarial or domestic roles and men always perform authority and leadership roles.

---

[10] A build screen is a technique in CBT where information appears on the screen one thought at a time. Build screens help students focus on one piece of information at a time, absorb it, and then receive additional information. Presenting a full screen of complex information at one time can decrease the amount of information students retain.

Text

1. Use initial capitalization style for all text except for special words that demonstrate exactly how students will see them, such as special keys on a computer keyboard. Develop a standard way of identifying these special words.
2. The first time you use an abbreviation or an acronym in a lesson, spell the entire name of the acronym, followed by the abbreviation or acronym in parentheses. After the first use, you can use the acronym or abbreviation for the remainder of the lesson. All standard abbreviations are acceptable without spelling them out (i.e., a.m., p.m.).
3. Lists of items that are to be completed in a specified order should be numbered. Simple lists can be bulleted.
4. Use a standard way to write numbers that can be found in any style guide.

Grammar

1. Avoid using masculine or feminine pronouns — he/she.
2. Use third person or the implied "you" to avoid becoming too informal or chatty.
3. Use present tense for lesson content, future tense for objectives, past tense for summaries, and present tense for test questions.
4. Always use active voice. It is clearer, more concise, and more direct than passive.
5. Indefinite pronouns (it, that, these, those, etc.) should be followed by the word the pronoun represents or clearly refer back to some concept or idea. Avoid using indefinite pronouns if the meaning becomes unclear.
6. Using "that" or "which" — always use "that" unless the phrase is set off by commas to indicate that it is parenthetical.

> For example:
> - The wrench that you use to fix the part is found in your tool kit.
> - The wrench, which can be found in your tool kit, is the one used to fix the part. [parenthetical phrase used as a reminder of where the wrench can be found]

Editing Symbols

Use the editing symbols your group is comfortable with. These can be found in any style guide. The symbols you use are not as important as being sure that everyone knows what they are, uses them, and can interpret them.

RATIONALE

The Course Design and Development Specification standards that govern the design and development of CBT products will also be used by an evaluation team to conduct formative evaluation reviews of the materials. There are typically teams of designers and developers working on a project, all of whom have different writing styles. The purpose of the Course Design and Development

Specification is to make the final product appear as if one person created it even though most projects use multiple designers and developers. The final product will better facilitate learning through its consistency, logical construction, and flow.

APPLICATION TOOLS

The writing standards that you develop should be included in a Course Design and Development Specification document. The outline for a Course Design and Development Specification is the aggregate of all the information in this Unit.

The formative evaluation forms that you use to review the Unit and Lesson Designs are found in the Application Tools section of Chapter 3-6.

CHAPTER 3-2
INFORMATION STRUCTURE

INTRODUCTION

Information that is presented in a course can be divided into five major categories, called presentation strategies (concepts, processes, procedures, principles, and facts). Each strategy has a unique way that it should be presented.

WHAT TO DO

Your first task is to decide which presentation strategy to use to present your information. Here are the names and definitions for each of the strategies.

Concepts

Concepts are classes of objects, events, or elements that have common characteristics along with a common name. They systematically classify phenomena into categories defined by the attributes of the concept.

Processes

Processes explain how things work rather than how to do things. The ISD Process is an example. It systematically explains an approach to produce instructional materials.

Procedures

Procedures explain how to do things. They are a set of sequential, ordered steps that are performed to accomplish a task. (For example, what we are attempting to do in this book is add step-by-step procedures to the ISD process so that you can complete the design and development of a CBT project.)

Principles

Principles are readily accepted statements, tested through time, that show cause and effect relationships that result in predictable outcomes. Principles are guidelines; they are often used to solve complex problems that have a known algorithm. You may remember principles that you used to solve theorems in geometry. Other examples are principles of learning like reinforcement, motivation, and transfer of training.

Facts

Facts are items of specific information that show an arbitrary relationship between objects or events, such as names and labels. Facts cannot be generalized.

How To Do It

Here are suggestions on how to implement presentation strategies.

Concepts

You should teach concepts using definitions, examples, and analogies.

Provide practice using discrimination activities between examples and non-examples; begin with those that are easy to discriminate and move toward those that are more difficult. End with a situation where students are required to make the correct choice from a set of possible choices.

```
EASY➜➜➜➜➜➜➜➜➜➜➜➜➜ DIFFICULT
SPECIFIC➜➜➜➜➜➜➜➜➜➜➜➜➜GENERAL
```

Support your instruction and practice with pictures, graphic representations, charts, and videos.

Processes

Teach processes using tables, flowcharts, simulations, and animation to show the dynamics of the process (i.e., how one aspect affects another). The High Level Course Flowchart (Figure 3-4-1) is an example.

If understanding a process will help the student understand a procedure, explain the process first. Use case studies, simulations, and work problems. Some people will argue that you do not need to know a process to be able to complete a procedure. That may be true; if you have only detailed steps to follow, you can complete a procedure if you follow those steps exactly. Teaching someone to follow instructions only works where there is no need to think. The majority of procedures require — or at least **should** require — some degree of thought or judgment. Support instruction of processes with pictures and charts.

Procedures

Teach procedures using demonstrations that students can watch and then duplicate, action/decision tables, and displays that list steps.

Support instruction with guided practice, then simulations, and finally hands-on activities.

```
DEMONSTRATION➜GUIDED PRACTICE➜SIMULATION➜PERFORMANCE
```

Principles

Teach principles using the principle itself and the guidelines for the principle. Provide examples in context, demonstrations, and displays of information.

For example:

> A principle of learning states that "Students learn best when there is transfer of training."
> - A guideline for this principle is: "teach information in as close to the actual context that information will be used so that students can clearly see the relationship to the workplace."
> - An example you could provide to support the principle might be "when teaching listening skills, show situations where people are using the skill followed by simulated role-playing situations where students practice the skill by viewing a scenario and finding the key points that characterize those listening skills."

Support instruction with video demonstrations, computer simulations, hands-on practice, and group discussion. You will have to go offline from the computer for discussions and hands-on activities, but let the computer do the initial training or, use very complicated branching that will respond to students in such a way as to simulate discussion.

Facts

Teach facts as textual information using color, special fonts, or indentations to call attention to them.

Practice facts by using job aids or providing exercises that require students to apply facts to the task being taught.

Support instruction with job aids or mnemonic devices, diagrams, and wall charts.

RATIONALE

The specifications that govern the design and development of the CBT will be used to conduct formative evaluation reviews of the materials. Following these specifications will make the final product appear as if one person created it even though most projects use multiple designers and developers. The final product will better facilitate learning through its consistency, logical construction, and flow.

APPLICATION TOOLS

The standards for structuring information that you develop should be included in a Course Design and Development Specification document. The outline for a Course Design and Development Specification is the aggregate of all the information in this Unit.

The formative evaluation forms that you use to review the unit and lesson outlines and storyboards are in the Application Tools section of Chapter 3-6.

CHAPTER 3-3
LESSON STRUCTURE

INTRODUCTION

CBT lessons should be structured in a consistent manner. This structure provides students with an effective learning environment where they can learn comfortably. Lesson structure should follow principles of learning that have been determined to be effective in presenting and learning information.

WHAT TO DO

A well structured lesson should contain eleven essential instructional/learning events. Each topic within a lesson should be considered a mini-lesson and follow the same pattern.

1. Use an **advance organizer**.
2. Present the learning **objectives**.
3. Present the **content** of the lesson.
4. Provide **guided practice** on small chunks of each topic.
5. Provide **feedback** on student activity.
6. Use **transitions** between topics.
7. **Summarize**.
8. Provide **independent practice** on the entire topic or concept of the lesson.
9. **Test** for the attainment of the concept.
10. **Remediate** (if the student does not demonstrate mastery).
11. **Retest**.

HOW TO DO IT

1. **Advance Organizer** — The advance organizer should be in the form of an audio and/or video introduction that explains what was previously learned, what will be learned in this lesson, and how both connect with each other and to subsequent learning. Include the purpose of the lesson and its relevance to the course. The advance organizer should answer the question "Why should I learn this?"

2. **Objectives** — The objectives tell the students what they will be able to do or what they will know as a result of completing a lesson. Present the objectives in an informal/conversational manner. Using second person, "you" is appropriate in this case.

3. **Content** — Presenting the content involves the use of the presentation strategies (see Chapter 3-2).

4. **Guided Practice** — Guided practice requires taking the information being trained and breaking it down into logical "chunks." These chunks can be practiced by students and they can receive immediate and corrective feedback

on how well they are doing or what to do differently. Guided practice reinforces a chunk of the content.

5. **Feedback** — Intersperse positive and corrective feedback throughout each lesson. Use the suggestions in the General Presentation Style section of Chapter 3-1.
   - **Positive** feedback tells students that they are correct and what comes next. Positive feedback may also include a statement telling the students why they are correct.
   - **Corrective** feedback tells the students that they were incorrect, and tells them what the correct answer is, to try again, or other action to take.

6. **Transitions** — Transitions appear between topics throughout the lesson. Transitions are mini-introductions that explain how what was just learned applies to the next topic.

7. **Summarize** — Summaries provide closure on a topic and remind the students what they learned.

8. **Independent Practice** — Independent practice for the student comes after completing the entire lesson, but before formal testing. Independent practice lets the students perform tasks in a manner as close to the actual work environment as possible. Students find out if they have followed the correct steps at the end of the practice. At the end of the entire practice, they should be given feedback on the points where they went wrong. Then, let them try again.

9. **Test** — Testing is covered in Chapter 3-8. Testing may occur online or offline, depending on the purpose of the training and the intended use of the results.

10. **Remediation** — Remediation is important because it provides clarification about why knowledge and skills are incorrectly learned, and presents the same information that should have been learned but in a different way. Remediation does not mean a rehash of the same material in the same way. Remediation usually means an abbreviated form of the initial instruction to help students pick up on points they might have missed.

11. **Retest** — Retesting follows remediation. It is used to determine if the students have now mastered the knowledge or skill. The same test as the first may be used. However it is better to use a parallel test. How to develop parallel forms of tests is covered in Unit 5, Evaluation.

RATIONALE

The specifications that govern the design and development of CBT will be used to conduct formative evaluation reviews of the materials. On most projects there are teams of designers and developers, all who have different presentation styles. The purpose is to make the final product look like one person created it.

APPLICATION TOOLS

The specifications for lesson structure that you develop should be included in a Course Design and Development Specification. The outline for a Course Design and Development Specification is the aggregate of all information in this Unit.

The formative evaluation forms that you use to review the Unit and Lesson Designs are found in the Application Tools section of Chapter 3-6.

CHAPTER 3-4
THE DETAILED COURSE OUTLINE

INTRODUCTION

Each lesson should have a Lesson Outline. This Lesson Outline is the basis for storyboarding lessons. Lesson Outlines roll up into Unit Outlines. All Unit and Lesson Outlines ultimately become part of a Detailed Course Outline.

WHAT TO DO

Be certain the Lesson Outline contains the following information:

1. A course flowchart with the lesson clearly identified.
2. A lesson flowchart.
3. A code that identifies the lesson number with respect to its association within the course. (Develop a system that works for you and follow it consistently.)
4. A lesson title.
5. Objectives for the lesson — the Terminal Objectives and the Lesson Objectives.
6. A lesson outline (find and consistently follow a standard outlining format).
7. Lesson length.
8. Weight of the lesson in the course (for testing purposes later, the weight of each lesson is important for considering how many questions to put in a final test).
9. The lesson introduction.
10. The information structure presentation strategy (see Chapter 3-2).
11. The testing strategy.
12. The lesson summary.
13. A list of the resources required to complete the lesson.
14. A list of the media to be used.

How To Do It

Course and Lesson Flowcharts

A course flowchart can be developed on any flowcharting software package. Some are easier to use than others. Experiment with several before deciding on one.

The High Level Course Flowchart shows the overall sequence of a course (see Figure 3-4-1). Detailed lesson flowcharts show the detail of branching with individual lessons. Figure 3-4-2 is an example of a detailed lesson flowchart.

Lesson Codes

You need to develop a coding system that will identify each lesson and its placement within the course with respect to the other lessons. You may want to keep this code in a database or use it as a programming reference. Certain DOS formats will restrict the number of letters/numbers/symbols you can use. A

Macintosh environment is not as restrictive. The important thing to remember is to use a code that is both simple and consistent.

You will want a different code for each part of the lesson (see Chapter 3-3). The programmer can use these codes to tell the computer where to branch to, establishing movement through the lesson and the course.

Lesson Title

Create a lesson title by which the lesson will be known. The programmer will use this title in the header and/or on the main menu for the course as the identifier for each lesson.

Terminal Objectives

List the terminal objective(s) for the lesson in the words and format that you decided upon for them to be seen on the screen. Remember, this format should be more conversational and not be in the formal style that you used when writing the objectives for the course.

Lesson Outline

Consistently follow a standard outlining format for the body of the lesson. These outlines are found in any style guide that is commercially available.

Lesson Length

Determine how long it will take for the person who uses all of the branching, reviews, tests, etc., to complete the lesson. Timing is important because each lesson contributes to the overall course, which has a predetermined length based on the analysis or customer requirements.

Lesson Weight

The weight of the lesson is determined by two major factors. The first, and most critical, is the importance of the lesson with respect to learning the content of the entire course. The second is the length of the lesson compared to the overall length of the course. You need to determine lesson weight because of its importance for testing purposes later — the weight of each lesson determines how many questions to put in a final test and affects the overall grading procedure. A process for weighting lessons is covered in Chapter 5-3.

Lesson Introduction

Write the lesson introduction just as you want to see and hear it in the lesson. If what students will hear (audio) and see (text) are different, then you will have to write the audio script as well as the text. Chapter 3-7 covers writing audio scripts.

Figure 3-4-1
High Level Course Flowchart

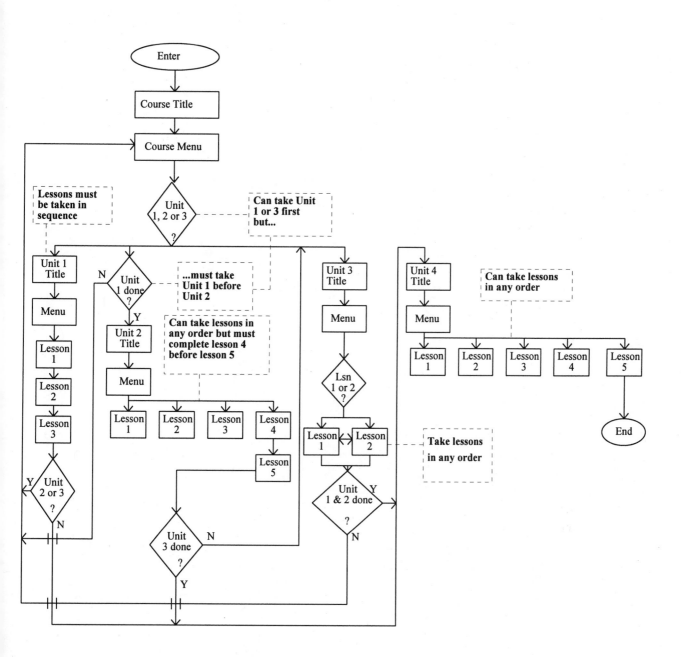

Figure 3-4-2
Detailed Lesson Flowchart

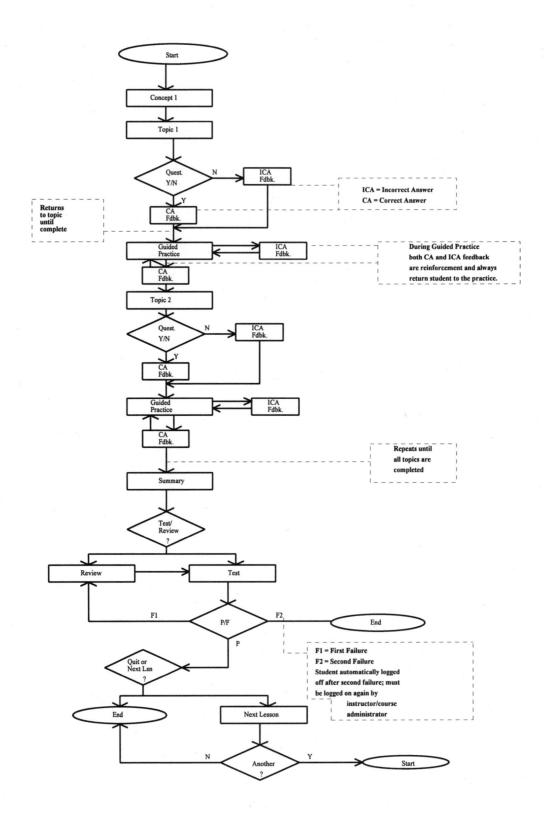

Structural Presentation Method

Along with the information that you intend to present, detail what presentation strategy must be used and tell the programmer how to develop it. Information Structuring was covered in Chapter 3-2.

Testing Strategy

Chapter 3-8 explains how to develop a testing strategy. Remember to include all questions for lessons, units, and the course when you write the Detailed Course Outline.

Lesson Summary

Create a summary of the lesson by following the same steps that you did for the introduction.

Resources Required

These may be offline instructional tools that will supplement the lesson (i.e., User's Guide, Student Manual, Course Administrator Guide). Include any resources other than the computer that the students need to complete the lesson.

Media

The Lesson Outline should state the media that will best demonstrate the information. Use the visualization suggestions in Chapter 3-2 to decide how you should present media. Go one step further and state if the visualization should be a graphic, motion video, still video, animation, etc. — whatever will fulfill the visualization requirement for the type of information you are presenting.

RATIONALE

The course design standards that govern the design and development of the products of the CBT will be used to conduct formative evaluation reviews of the materials. On most projects there are teams of designers and developers, all of whom have different writing styles. The purpose is to make the final product look like one person created it.

APPLICATION TOOLS

The formative evaluation forms that you use to review the Unit and Lesson Designs are found in the Application Tools section of Chapter 3-6. The following outline in Figure 3-4-4 shows the format for a Unit and Lesson Outline that results from the Design Phase.

Figure 3-4-3
Detailed Course Outline

I. Introductory Material
  A. The Job Description of the persons for whom the course is written.
  B. Reference Documents that are associated with the Lesson Outline Report.
  C. Purpose of the Unit and Lesson Outline.
II. Description of Each Unit
  A. Unit Number and Title
  B. Unit Length
    1. Online computer time
    2. Offline time (reading, laboratory exercises)
III. Unit Cross Reference Matrix
  A. Objective Number
  B. The Objective
  C. Type of Learning Required
  D. Media
  E. Instructional Strategy
  F. Testing Strategy
IV. Unit Content Outline
  A. Objectives
  B. Presentation
  C. Practice
  D. Evaluation
  E. Instructional Materials
  F. Resource Requirements
  G. Unit Tests
V. Matrix for Each Lesson
  A. Objective Number
  B. The Objective
  C. Type of Learning Required
  D. Media
  E. Instructional Strategy
  F. Testing Strategy
VI. Lesson Content Outline
  A. Objectives
  B. Presentation
  C. Guided Practice
  D. Independent Practice
  E. Common Errors of Performing Tasks in the Lesson
  F. Instructional Materials
  G. Resource Requirements
  H. Title of each Lesson
  I Lesson Length
  J. Introduction
  K. Information Structure(s)
  L. Lesson Quiz
  M. Evaluation
VII. Course Test

CHAPTER 3-5
DESIGNING THE USER INTERFACE

INTRODUCTION

The CBT user interface is critical to the success of any CBT course. There is nothing else to keep the student interested in learning except the computer. Therefore, the user interface should always keep the audience in mind. Decisions should include:

(1) the level of simplicity or complexity you can ask the students to perform (based on what the students' experience with computers have been in the past);

(2) screen layout; and

(3) the interaction between the students and the computer.

WHAT TO DO

The Student

Always keep your audience in mind. The methods that students must use to maneuver through the course should never interfere with learning. The best answer you can get to the question "What did you think of the way the computer branched?" is "I didn't notice it."

Screen Layout

Include the following considerations in your screen layout and design:

- Consistent placement of information.
- Colors/color combinations.
- Object size.

Interactivity

Keep the lesson as interactive as possible. Keep the student involved in the learning process. You accomplish this by having the student input information, requiring him or her to think about the answer, at various points. There should be an interaction every three to five screens with a maximum of seven screens before there is an interaction. (Interactivity does *not* mean simply pressing the <Enter> key to move the computer program to the next screen.)

HOW TO DO IT

Considering The User

Your Audience Analysis told you the characteristics of the users of the CBT course. As you design, be specifically aware of how much computer experience the students have had. The interface should be transparent to the students, allowing them to move easily through the course without having the computer interface interfere with their learning. Unnecessary levels of menus and decisions about paths to take will actually interfere with learning.

Convey one message or event per screen.

Use the computer to do what it does best: demonstrate, provide practice, test, and give immediate feedback.

Consistent Placement of Information

Keep the screens as consistent as possible from section to section. Each screen type should have its own look that students can get used to. For example, have one Main Menu for the course and then a topic menu for each section. These menus (shown in Figure 3-5-1) should always look the same with respect to color, position of text on screen, headings, and function.

Figure 3-5-2 is an example of a Question Screen.

General Guidelines

In general:
- Limit the number of words per line of text to 10 or 12.
- Limit the number of lines per screen to 14 or 16.
- Frame text with a simple border.
- Leave at least a one inch margin between the text and the border.
- Use a text font and size that is easy to read.
- Keep a "paragraph" on one screen.

Use a consistently placed and formatted header. This header should have the name of the lesson on it and be on the top of the screen. You should include some indication on it of where the student is in within the course, such as Introduction, Objectives, Lesson, Practice, Test, Summary, or Review.

Put a page number or other progress indicator in the bottom left corner of every screen to let the student know how far into each lesson he or she is (in all cultures in which people normally read from left to right). Other mechanisms might be a color bar that progressively changes color or lengthens as students move through the lesson.

You can also use color coding to let students know how far into a course they are. For example, gray out or change the color of those lessons on the main menu that students have completed.

Use textual titles as guides such as "Lesson Menu" above lesson menu screens, "Question" for question screens, etc. (This is in the same framed area of the screen as the other text — not in the header.)

Figure 3-5-1
Menu Screen

Managing in a Team Environment — Lesson
Menu Selections

Lesson Menu

1   Role of the Manager

2   Role of the Supervisor

3   Role of the Employee

4   Return to Main Menu

Choice: ___

Make your selection. Then press Enter.

[ ]Page Number   O O O O (Student Controls)

Figure 3-5-2
Question Screen

The User Interface — Quiz
Menu Selections

Question

1. The most important person to keep in mind when designing a
   user interface is _____.

    A. the programmer.

    B. your customer.

    C. the course developer.

    D. the end user.

Choice: _Δ_ (Blinking cursor will be on this line)
Type the letter of your answer. Then press Enter.

[ ]Page Number   O O O O (Student Controls)

Figure 3-5-3
Preferences for Instructional Information

Lesson Title — Section
Menu Selections

First Preferred
Position

Third Preferred
Position

Second Preferred
Position

Least Preferred
Position

Fourth Preferred
Position

[ ]Page Number   ○ ○ ○   ○ (Student Controls)

In many languages (including English), reading requires eye movement from top to bottom and left to right. The sample screen in Figure 3-5-3 shows the preferred placement of instructional information on the screen.

You must decide what content of the screen is most important when deciding where to place information. Here are some guidelines:
- If you want students to read the text then study a visual, put the text on the left and the visual representation on the right.
- If you want students to see a demonstration and then read text, put the visual on the left and the text on the right.
- If you only have a video screen with audio, use the entire screen and center the video.
- If you have only a text screen, center the text.

Be sure that you have all screen components (headers, numbering, control buttons) visible at all times. For example, you may have control buttons that allow students to move to the next screen, move backward, stop video or audio, etc. The program may not always allow students to stop the video — for example, when there is only a text screen or a still video — but you should still have the control visible on the screen. You should change the control to a different color or dim it when it is not active or available so that students know when it will and will not function.

Prompt boxes, such as the one that follows, tell students that they have to perform a certain action to get the program to proceed. Prompts should always appear in the center of the screen, in a colored box, with a concise heading and a very brief message instructing the student what to do. When the student takes the correct action, the prompt box should disappear.

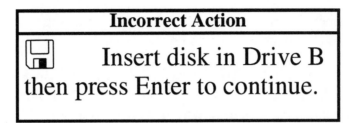

Colors are very important when considering the user interface. You will want to experiment with background and text colors during prototyping to find a suitable combination. Have programmers and graphic artists develop a set of screens using different colors and have several students evaluate the screens. Some colors that look fine for a minute or two can become very hard on the eyes after seeing those colors repeated over 15 minutes. Remember to have people view several screens for at least 10 minutes before registering their reactions.

Use the following guidelines for colors. In general, use cool colors (such as amber or blue) for background screens because these are easy on the eyes. The best foreground color on amber is black; on a blue field, black or white work quite well.

Use hot colors (red, green) only for warnings or danger messages. **Never** use red **on** green — about 10% of the general population of men (condition is *extremely* rare in women) cannot see anything on this combination because they are color blind.

Interactivity

Meaningful

Make interactions meaningful. You should not insert a question or ask students for responses just to have inputs. If your learning events are short and confined to one screen, you can ask students to input a response to an embedded question at intervals of three to five screens.

When you ask questions, allow students a second input if their first is incorrect. Provide feedback on all interactions. Remember, the purpose of interactivity is to keep students meaningfully involved and learning.

Input Methods

There are various input methods that you can use. Keyboard, touch screen, mouse, trackball, light pen, and voice are all forms of input. The keyboard is the most traditional form of input. Given the average user of your CBT lessons, you might want to provide more than one input option.

Touch screens are monitors with touch sensitive areas that, when touched with a finger or other object, register an input.

A mouse or trackball is a device that controls (moves) an on-screen cursor, sometimes called a pointer, to a desired location. There is a button on the mouse/trackball that you click when the cursor is positioned over the desired object on the screen. Clicking the button registers the input.

A light pen is a beam of light that, when shone on a light-sensitive area of the screen, registers an input.

Interactivity can also be achieved through audio (voice) inputs. Although the application of this technology is limited in training applications at the time of the printing of this book, it offers exciting options for future courseware development.

You should decide what input method(s) will be appropriate for your students. For example, persons who lack control of their hands will find it difficult to use a traditional keyboard for inputs. Requiring long answers that these students must type will take far too long and reduce the effectiveness of their learning. There are specialized adaptive devices such as keyboards with large keys that are easier to strike. Light pens can be placed into a head band and the user can direct the light beam at the screen. The more complex the input form, the higher the cost involved, but student capabilities should always dictate the input method.

Learner Control

Whenever reading on-screen text is required, the text must remain on the screen until the student makes an input — either to continue or record an answer to a question. The only exception might be during a simulation of computer software which contains screens that "time-out" thereby limiting the time available to input responses.

Learner Guidance

Students should know what to do at every step of the way throughout a CBT lesson or course. This guidance comes in the form of everything from menus to prompts, to feedback on questions. Guidance can also be contained in online dictionaries and Help Menus.

Menus tell students where they are, where they have been, and where they are going. Prompts tell students when they have entered a correct/incorrect input, waited too long to make an input, or, in general, direct students to do something that moves them through the lesson or course. Feedback for questions might tell students to try again.

Dictionaries provide information about specialized terms that are important or that must be learned. Online dictionaries can be very helpful and can be as simple as defining terms or as complicated as giving students pictures and diagrams of the terms.

Help Menus provide information on functional aspects of the course that students might use infrequently. For instance, a student may not remember how to use the online dictionary. A Help option should also include instructions on how to use the Help menu.

"Hot spot" is a term used to indicate a sensitive area on the screen that, when selected in some way (pointing to with the cursor and pressing the <Enter> key or a click of the mouse, touch screen, light pen), will move the computer program to another area where there is more information. The hot spots may be indicated by a different color (i.e., a word in text may be highlighted or have a different color background or there may be boxes around certain portions of a graphic that, when selected, will show an expanded view of the area).

Programmer's Guide

There should also be programming specifications but these are specific to the programming language or the authoring system. The development team should create a Programmer's Guide (see Figure 3-5-4 for outline) for authors to use when authoring lessons.

RATIONALE

The specifications that govern the design and development of CBT are used to conduct formative evaluation reviews of the materials. On most projects there are teams of designers and developers, all who have different presentation styles. The purpose is to make the final product look like one person created it.

APPLICATION TOOLS

The storyboarding standards that you develop should be included in a CDS document. The outline for a CDS document is the aggregate of all the information in this Unit. The formative evaluation forms that you use to review the Unit and Lesson Designs and storyboards are in the Application Tools section of Chapter 3-6.

Figure 3-5-4
Programmer's Guide Outline

1.   File Naming Conventions   *[Specific alphanumeric identification system to save and recall files.]*

2.   Various Screen Types   *[Details of the content of various screen types.]*

   - Question (and all the variations — Multiple Choice, Matching, True/False, Completion, etc.)
   - Menu
   - Graphic
   - Animation

3.   Various Screen Functions   *[Details of the use and purpose of various capabilities.]*

   - Cross Referencing (screens with hot spots)
   - Branching
   - Video

4.   Specialized File Requirements   *[Specialized information peculiar to the authoring system or programming language.]*

   - size limitations
   - storing information
   - calling and integrating various types of files

CHAPTER 3-6
STORYBOARDING AND REVIEW CYCLES

INTRODUCTION

Storyboards are developed from the Lesson Outline. You must describe or show the visual, audio, and programming portion of the storyboard. There is an example of a storyboard format in the Application Tools section of this chapter. You should design one that fits your specific needs; however, you need all of the components that we list in the example.

Use the elements of course design standards listed in previous chapters to develop your storyboards. Keep in mind the consistent position of certain elements on the screen. These consistent elements must be determined by you and your team of instructional designers and developers. Some general guidelines are listed here and in Chapter 3-5.

Your CDS should include your review cycles and how to track and control versions and revisions of the courseware.

WHAT TO DO

You must have standards that govern developing the storyboard. The best way is to develop a template that contains a visual box that will simulate the requirements for the number of words per line and number of lines per screen. This will take some experimentation during prototyping. Type some text in a certain size font on the storyboard and then have a course developer program the text. Compare the font on the screen against the standard. Adjust the size of the font on the visual area of the storyboard until you have a match between the storyboard and the screen.

You need to establish review cycles for storyboards. Include a technical review, an instructional review, a standards review, an editorial review, and a management review. Each of these review cycles is explained on the form for each found in the Application Tools section of this chapter.

Screen numbering conventions are important because most programming languages or authoring systems reference screen numbers for branching. These conventions must be worked out between the design team (for the CDS) and the course developers (for the Programmer's Guide).

How To Do It

Developing The Storyboard

It is important that everyone use the standards that have been developed regarding size and type of font, text, and colors when creating the storyboards.

Remember to make accommodations in your numbering system for storyboards that may have to be added later. Decimals are often used to allow for further additions.

For example, one numbering scheme for each lesson might be :

001	Title Screen
002 - 005	Introduction
010 - 015	Objectives
100 - 500	Content
600 - 610	Summary
650 - 700	Review
800 - 900	Test

RATIONALE

The course design standards that govern the creation of storyboards will be used to conduct formative evaluation reviews of the materials. On most projects there are teams of designers and developers, all of whom have different presentation styles. The purpose is to make the final product look like one person created it.

APPLICATION TOOLS

This section provides many tools that you can use to perform the tasks required for storyboard review cycles. Figure 4-3-4 in the chapter on Post Production is a scheduling form for use of the computer. You will need a form similar to this one to use for Configuration Control during these review cycles.

Figure 3-6-1
Storyboard Template

STORYBOARD

LESSON TITLE: SEQUENCE NUMBER: _____

SECTION:

VISUAL:

AUDIO:

PROGRAMMING:

BRANCHING: Previous _____ Next _____ Variable _____
TYPE: _____ VIDEO IN _____ VIDEO OUT _____
FILES REQUIRED: Graphic _____ Audio _____

Figure 3-6-2
Explanation of Storyboard Template

LESSON TITLE: Title of the lesson as it appears on the screen in the Header.

SEQUENCE NUMBER: A running, sequential, page number.

SECTION: The section "Introduction," "Objectives," "Lesson," "Summary," "Quiz," "Test."

VISUAL: Describes what the student will see on the screen. This can be described in words or with an illustration. Text and questions should be in the identical or corresponding font and size that students will see on the screen.

AUDIO: Any narration that the student will hear. This can be listed here or referenced to audio scripts. (Write the scripts that accompany the screen on separate pages and attach these pages immediately behind the storyboard screen.)

PROGRAMMING: Any special instructions to the author (including correct answers to question screens). Most standard programming instructions will be in the Programmer's Guide and do not need to be mentioned in this section.

BRANCHING: Explains where the program goes after a student input. This is expressed using the storyboard number.

Previous: Where the program goes if the student goes backward.

Next: Where the program goes if the student uses <Continue> to move linearly forward.

Variable: A series of if/then statements for variable branching. For example, if the student answers a question correctly, the program moves one screen; if incorrectly, the branching moves to a different screen in the program.

TYPE: The type of screen (i.e., graphic — text is normally considered graphic depending on how it is created on the screen — or video).

THE FOLLOWING ARE COMPLETED BY THE AUTHOR

VIDEO IN: Identifies the video file number where video begins on the videodisc or CD ROM.

VIDEO OUT: Identifies the video file number where the video ends.

FILES REQUIRED: Files from other sources (i.e., graphic, audio, CD ROM).

Graphic: Diagrams, drawing, etc., that reside on the computer software disk but must be called up.

Audio: Logged audio file numbers that must be called up from audio source.

Figure 3-6-3
Editorial Review Directions

An Editorial Review ensures consistency within and between lessons in course materials. The thoroughness of an Editorial Review enhances the learning of the student through the improved overall flow and consistency of the product.

REVIEW PROCEDURES

The Course Design Specification is the guide to conducting the review of the following elements:

1. Correct spelling

2. Correct punctuation

3. Correct grammar
   - Person and number
   - Tense
   - Noun/verb agreement

4. Voice

Recording Errors

A. Record each error you observed on the document where you saw it.

B. If reviewing an online lesson, record the error on the Online Lesson Review Form.

Figure 3-6-4
Editorial Review Form

PROJECT _____ LESSON _____ DATE _____

Reviewer's Signature _____

Be sure that you identify any unique specifications in the space provided. At the completion of your review, check each item to certify that your review included each item.

__ 1. Correct Spelling
     List any words that have unique form.

     _____
     _____
     _____
     _____
     _____

__ 2. Correct Punctuation.
     List any special punctuation specifications.

     _____
     _____
     _____
     _____

__ 3. Correct Grammar
     List any specifications regarding:
        • Person _____
        • Number _____
        • Tense _____
        • Noun/Verb agreement _____

__ 4. Voice
     List any unique specifications regarding voice.

     _____
     _____
     _____

Figure 3-6-5
Instructional Review Directions

An Instructional Review ensures consistency within and between lessons in course materials. The thoroughness of an Instructional Review enhances the learning of the student through the improved overall instructional integrity of the product.

REVIEW PROCEDURES

The Course Design Specification is the guide to conducting the review of the following elements:

1. Readability
    - Written at the appropriate grade level for the audience as determined from the audience analysis.
    - Register[11] (i.e., formal: highly stylized and impersonal; consultative: instructive and semi-formal; informal: casual).
2. Vocabulary
    - Spoken using terms and vocabulary appropriate for the audience as determined from the Audience Analysis.
    - Register (i.e., formal: highly stylized and impersonal; consultative: instructive and semi-formal; informal: casual).
3. Transitions
    - The lesson ties previous topics to current topics.
4. Conceptual Framework
    - The lesson contains these events of learning:
        - Introduces the lesson in a way that relates the current lesson to previous and subsequent lessons.
        - States the objectives.
        - Presents the content by introducing an overview of each topic, breaks the topic into component parts, and ties all components together in a summary.
        - Checks often for understanding and provides feedback to learners.
        - Provides guided practice where applicable.
        - Provides independent practice.
5. Congruence
    - There is a natural flow of information:
        - Objectives

---

[11] Register is the level of formality or informality of the writing style used in the CBT lessons. Very formal register is third person singular or plural using passive voice to a great extent. Casual register uses very familiar language, first person singular or plural or the person's name (which can be captured when the student logs on to the course the first time and programmed using variables so that the name will appear at certain places in the course).

  – Topics associated with the objectives
  – Topics summarized
  – Topics reviewed
  – Topics tested
6. Question Format/Feedback
   • Questions reference the correct objective:
     – Quiz questions reference a Lesson Objective.
     – Test questions reference a Terminal Objective.
   • Questions are in the correct format.
7. Mapping Strategies
   • All strategies are correctly mapped.
     – Processes
     – Procedures
     – Concepts
     – Principles
     – Facts

Recording Errors

A. Record each error you observed on the document where you saw it.

Figure 3-6-6
Instructional Review Form

PROJECT _____ LESSON _____ DATE _____

Reviewer's Signature _____

Be sure that you identify any unique specifications in the space provided. At the completion of your review, check each item to certify that your review included each item.

__ 1. Readability [Expected Level _____]
   • Written at the appropriate grade level for the audience as determined from the Audience Analysis.
   • Register

__ 2. Vocabulary
   • Spoken
   • Register

__ 3. Transitions

__ 4. Conceptual Framework

__ 5. Congruence

__ 6. Question Format

__ 7. Question Feedback

__ 8. Questions Reference the Correct Objective

__ 9. All Instruction is Correctly Mapped

Figure 3-6-7
Standards Review Directions

A Standards Review ensures consistency within and between lessons in course materials. The thoroughness of a Standards Review enhances the learning of the student through the improved overall quality of the product.

REVIEW PROCEDURES

The Course Design Specification is the guide to conducting the review of the following elements:

1. Standard Screen Elements
   - All standard areas of the screens are in the correct position, using correct fonts.

2. Standard Screen Specifications
   - All standardized screens are used in the correct place and are identical in appearance.

3. Standard Screen Colors
   - All color standards are adhered to.

4. Text
   - Standards for text size are adhered to.

5. Standard Reference Terminology
   - All informational areas of the document are completed.
   - Scripting conventions are observed.
       — Phonetic spelling guide
       — Referencing builds
       — Writing numerals
       — Video references

6. Recording conventions are adhered to.
   - Correct use of narrators.
   - Consistent audio levels.

Recording Errors

A. Record each error you observed on the document where you saw it.
B. If reviewing an online lesson, record the error on the Online Lesson Review Form.

Figure 3-6-8
Standards Review Form

PROJECT _____ LESSON _____ DATE _____

Reviewer's Signature _____

Be sure that you identify any unique specifications in the space provided. At the completion of your review, check each item to certify that your review included this item.

__ 1. Standard Screen Elements
   • All standard areas of the screen are in the correct position and use the correct fonts.

__ 2. Standard Screen Specifications
   • All standardized screens are used in the correct place and are identical in appearance.

__ 3. Standard Screen Colors
   • All color standards are adhered to.

__ 4. Text
   • Standards for text size are adhered to.

__ 5. Standard Reference Terminology

__ 6. Recording conventions are adhered to.

Figure 3-6-9
Technical Review Directions

A Technical Review ensures consistency within and between lessons in course materials. The thoroughness of a Technical Review enhances the learning of the student through the improved overall accuracy of the product.

REVIEW PROCEDURES

The Course Design Specification is the guide to conducting the review of the following elements:

1. All topics required to thoroughly teach the lesson are covered.

2. All topics are covered in the order they should be presented.

3. All topics are covered to the proper depth considering the audience.

4. All technical terms are accurate and complete as listed in the documentation for the course.

5. All technical terms are spelled correctly.

Recording Errors

A. Record each error you observed on the document where you saw it.

Figure 3-6-10
Technical Review Form

PROJECT _____ LESSON _____ DATE _____

Reviewer's Signature _____

Be sure that you identify any unique specifications in the space provided. At the completion of your review, check each item below to certify that your review included all items.

__ 1.   All topics required to thoroughly teach the lesson are covered.

__ 2.   All topics are covered in the order they are listed.

__ 3.   All topics are covered to the proper depth considering the audience.

__ 4.   All technical terms are accurate and complete as listed in the documentation for the course.

__ 5.   All technical terms are spelled correctly.

Figure 3-6-11
Management Review Directions

A Management Review ensures the adherence to the contractual requirements of the project. Adherence to contract requirements affirms the quality of the final product in meeting the needs of the customer.

REVIEW PROCEDURE

Use the contract prepared for the project as a guide to conducting the review of the following elements of the materials:

1. The materials conform to the requirements outlined in the contract.

2. The materials conform to the requirements of the system specification.

Recording Errors

A. Record each error you observed on the document where you saw it.

Figure 3-6-12
Management Review Form

PROJECT _____ LESSON _____ DATE _____

Reviewer's Signature _____

At the completion of your review, check each item to certify that your review included each item.

__ 1.   The materials conform to the requirements outlined in the contract.

__ 2.   The materials conform to the requirements of the system specification.

Figure 3-6-13
Online Lesson Review Form

PROJECT _____ LESSON # _____ SCREEN # _____

Instructions: Each reviewer must initial comments and clearly identify the problem or error. Also initial and date when error is corrected and verified.

Reviewer (initial)	Problem/Error	Corrected by: (initial)	Date Corrected	Verified Corrected (initial)	Date Verified

CHAPTER 3-7
AUDIO AND VIDEO

INTRODUCTION

The multimedia capabilities of the computer allow you to enhance the ways that students learn, using varied combinations of audio and video.

WHAT TO DO

There are decisions at several levels regarding audio and video:

1. When and how much to use.
2. How to call for them in your standards.

Audio and video production are expensive. The budget will, in many instances, dictate how much audio and video you can use. For example, an industry standard for good quality commercial video can be as high as $2000 per finished minute. A small project can have a major portion of its budget devoured quickly by video.

Disk space is another consideration. Videodiscs are limited to about one hour of video per disc (1/2 hour per side). CD ROM is much more accommodating. You can get about six hours of video, audio, and graphics on one CD ROM. CD ROMs are also inexpensive to reproduce. The cost is also a good reason to use this medium if you have courseware that might require changes over time.

Audio and video require written scripts, casting, developing shot lists, set design, set construction, lighting, a database to track shots, and post production (such as editing, producing masters, and pressing videodiscs and/or CD ROMs).

How much is a minute of video or audio in the writing of the scripts and storyboards? Here are some estimates that seem to be pretty consistent:
- Approximately 1-1/3 pages of script for each minute of audio.
- Approximately 2 pages of script for each minute of video.

If you count the number of pages and use these estimates you can approximate how much audio and video you have included in a course. Some courses require very little, while others would be ehanced considerably through the use of extensive audio and video. You many need to adjust the amount of each depending on your budget. How much and where audio and video will be used are decisions that must be made at this time.

Audio

Audio involves three major components:

- Voice Over is that audio narration that overlays text, graphics, and video; spoken by an off-screen actor or narrator.
- Scripts are written for scenarios acted out by on-screen talent.
- Sound effects are those sounds — natural and computer-generated —that enhance the audio and attract attention to certain aspects of the lesson.

Video

Video consists of:

- **Motion** video is a continuous running video sequence used to demonstrate or test a concept or procedure.
- **Still** video is a sequence stopped on one frame to point out a step or event that needs particular attention.
- **Stop motion** video is a series of still video frames that progress at a certain rate to demonstrate a sequence. Stop motion is used when the actual full motion sequence would take a long sequence to demonstrate and there is no advantage to seeing the entire thing — only specific points that need to have attention drawn to them.

Graphics

Graphics are any type of computer generated images that represent or make a point about a concept. Diagrams may be sketches or detailed representations of technical materials (also considered graphics in that they are computer generated). Animation shows movement and directs attention to aspects that are not easily seen by using video.

How To Do It

Components Of Standards

The Programmer's Guide should provide information to the programmer on how to integrate and call up video. This guide should also tell the video specialist how to log the audio and video so that the programmer can access it from the videodisc or CD ROM when it is needed. For example, after the video check disc is pressed, it needs to be logged to identify the number sequence of the frames on the disc — where a sequence begins and where it ends. We will not cover these aspects of video production and post production here, since they are more appropriately covered in specialized texts for programmers and audio and video specialists.

What we will give you are some guidelines on how to describe shots on storyboards and scripts so that the video producer will know what you require. Basically, however, the storyboard designer should act as the technical advisor with respect to setting up the shots. That way the designers can see that they are getting what they had conceived on the storyboard. Changes can be made on the spot, thus saving time and money for reshoots.

Standards should define the terms that the designer should use. These are available in any text on video production so they won't be defined here but here are the ones you should address:

Framing

1. Shots
   Extreme Long Shot (ELS)
   Long Shot (LS)
   Medium Shot (MS)
   Close Up (CU)
   Extreme Close Up (ECU)
2. Angle
   High
   Normal
   Low
3. View
   Front
   Left
   Right
   Head
   Top
   Bottom
   Combinations
4. Subjects
5. Video types (defined and explained in this chapter)
6. Camera Movements
   Pan
   Zoom
7. Description of the action

Your CDS should also list inappropriate uses of video that you want to avoid in your application. For example, do not try to show detail through video when a simple graphic would do it better; and eliminate video of someone talking on the screen (known as a "talking head") whenever audio overlay would be just as effective.

Audio

Voice Over

Use voice over to describe what is happening, about to happen, or did happen on the screen. Audio narration should support text, not duplicate it. It is very distracting for students to try to read text on a screen while it is being read to them.

Decide if narration should support text or if text should support narration. The support should be the shortest amount used. So, if you are going to support narration with text, the text should be bulleted items that appear on the screen as the narration makes a point about what is being viewed in the video. If there will only be text on a screen, with no video, use full text and no audio at all.

Dialog

In addition to your storyboards, you will need to create separate dialog scripts for on-screen talent to present scenarios and examples that students will view. These should be written on separate pages that are referenced on the storyboard. You will have to develop a numbering scheme for scripts to reference storyboards.

Scripts must be written in a format that can be used by talent and narrators. Scripts must list the name of the speakers, followed by what they say; state the actions that the actors must perform, and when; set the scene, the background, and the scenario around which the script is built.

Example:

THE SCENE:
[An office setting.]

THE ACTORS:
[Barbara Price — marketing manager]
[Allen Bowes — her secretary]

[Barbara is dressed in a business suit.]
[Allen is in a suit with a pencil behind his ear.]

BARBARA:
[Seated at her desk, she reaches for the intercom button and says...]

Hello, Allen, I have a letter I want you to take down in dictation.

ALLEN:
[Speaking from offstage, his voice sounds mechanically
reproduced as through the intercom]

Certainly, Ms. Price.

[Allen then enters from stage left with stenographer's pad in his hand, sits in the chair
across the desk from Barbara]

Ready when you are.

BARBARA:

Take a letter to Educational Technologies Consultants.

[Fadeout]

If voice over is part of a dialog script, it should be in the script, as well as on the storyboard.

RATIONALE

We have known for decades that there are several learning modalities. The true advantage of CBT is its ability to deliver instruction through both visual and auditory media to better meet the individualized learning needs of students.

Some of us learn best by seeing something (visual modality), others by hearing (auditory modality), still others by touching and doing (tactile/kinesthetic modality). These are all known as the VATK Method (Visual, Auditory, Tactile, Kinesthetic) of teaching and learning. You can review the literature and find numerous references to sensory modality learning. But all of the literature agrees that the best method of instruction is to use a combination of as many of the sensory modes of learning as possible.

The multisensory approach to instruction is a well established principle of learning. This fact is the one solid rationale for the use of CBT, especially CBT which makes extensive use of multimedia, thus justifying the use of audio and video.

APPLICATION TOOLS

The writing specifications that you developed should be included in a Course Design Specification. The outline for the CDS document is the aggregate of all the information in this unit.

The formative evaluation forms that you use to review the Unit and Lesson Outline and storyboards are in the Application Tools section of Chapter 3-6.

CHAPTER 3-8
QUESTIONING, TESTING, AND FEEDBACK

INTRODUCTION

This chapter provides information on how to test using CBT. Your analysis told you what type of test to use based on the purpose of the course, the students' needs, and skills required. We will examine the strengths and weaknesses of the various types of tests applied to various testing situations. We will discuss the development of essay tests, objective tests (multiple choice, completion/short answer, matching, true/false), simulations, and performance tests; when and where to use testing and questioning.

You need to determine the testing strategy in the Design Phase for three reasons:

(1) to include it in the Detailed Content Outline document;
(2) to outline it in the Unit Outline; and
(3) to include test questions in the Lesson Outline.

Some factors to consider in the testing strategy are:
* Can students test out of the units of the course?
* Is gain in knowledge important?
* How do you want to check progress in mastering the concepts in the course?
* What is the final measure of success?

WHAT TO DO

Table 3-8-1 outlines the types of questions to use in a course, and the placement, purpose, frequency, and the hierarchical level at which they should be written.

Tests and Their Application

There are numerous types of tests and test questions that you can construct for CBT courseware. Some have certain advantages over others. Remember, the ultimate decision on what type of testing to use is determined by the various forms of analysis (i.e., Instructional, Situational). Here are the various types of tests, with their advantages and disadvantages:

Essay Tests

Essay tests are used to provide students with the opportunity to fully express the depth of their knowledge on a topic or subject. Essay tests may involve short answers (of a few paragraphs) or extended essays (several pages). Essay questions require students to call upon all of their mental faculties to recall relevant information from all information they know on a topic, arrange the answer mentally, transfer that composition to paper or computer screen, or, in the case of oral exams, to formulate and express an answer. Essay questions can test the highest levels of the taxonomy but, because of their complexity, present certain drawbacks.

ADVANTAGES OF ESSAY TESTS

In general, these are the advantages of essay questions.

1. Effective in measuring complex learning such as integrating present knowledge to prior learning.
2. Easy to construct if appropriate guidelines are followed and firm scoring criteria are formed.
3. Emphasize integration of academic skills.
4. Eliminate guessing.

DISADVANTAGES OF ESSAY TESTS

The use of essay questions in CBT is somewhat restricted. In general, the disadvantages of essay questions are:

1. Difficult to score unless the instructor carefully maps out a scoring strategy (scores one question from all tests, sets up criteria for awarding points, in advance, is not unduly influenced by poor writing or knowing who the student is).
2. Scores are unreliable because it is difficult to maintain the same set of criteria from question to question.
3. Provides a limited sample of the instructional content because of the time required to compose and score answers.
4. Provides room for bluffing unless the instructor limits the length of the response and composes questions in such a way to structure the number of items the students can include.
5. Discriminates against those who have poor writing skills if writing is not the primary purpose of the test.

DIFFICULTIES OF USING ESSAY TESTS IN CBT

The problems for the use of essays in CBT are the problems in scoring by the computer as much as the design. You must provide the computer with the correct answer or answers through inputting variable strings into the computer. The computer then evaluates the inputs of the students and declares the answer correct or incorrect. The computer is completely impartial and can only interpret what is input. Therefore, you must include all possible acceptable answers for each key point in the variable string, the various ways that you will accept correct spelling, and how to assign points based on the key points mentioned.

You may decide, for very complicated material, that the time to construct and validate the test is not worth the information you will receive from it. We suggest using an essay only as a last resort in CBT if all other possible means of getting information is discussed and exhausted. The exception to this, of course, would be a writing course delivered through CBT.

Objective Tests: Multiple Choice

ADVANTAGES OF MULTIPLE CHOICE TESTS

1. Have the capability of measuring learning at all levels of the taxonomy by having students discriminate varying degrees of correctness.
2. Have the capability of minimizing guessing (although they do not eliminate it).
3. A lot of material can be sampled in a short amount of testing time.
4. Scoring is very objective.
5. Can easily perform test item analysis and distractor analysis.
6. Easy for the computer to interpret and score.

DISADVANTAGES OF MULTIPLE CHOICE TESTS

1. Time consuming to construct.
2. If not well written, may have more than one defensible correct answer.
3. If not well written, usually measure only low level knowledge and recall.
4. Indirectly measure skills; are not an accurate indicator of job performance.

Objective Tests: Matching

ADVANTAGES OF MATCHING TESTS

1. Easy to construct and score.
2. Ideal for measuring associations between facts.
3. Reduce the effects of guessing.

DISADVANTAGES OF MATCHING TESTS

1. May focus on trivial information.
2. Emphasize memorization.

Objective Tests: True/False, Yes/No, A/B

ADVANTAGES OF T/F TESTS

1. Useful where very factual information is being tested (embedded questions).
2. More information can be sampled when a lot of content has been covered.
3. Easy to score.

DISADVANTAGES OF T/F TESTS

1. Low level recall at the knowledge or comprehension level.
2. Fifty-fifty chance of guessing correctly.
3. Can only be used for information that is "absolute."
4. Difficult to write because the stems must be short but at the same time be clear enough to eliminate any ambiguity.

Objective Tests: Completion

ADVANTAGES OF COMPLETION TESTS
1. Easy to construct.
2. Guessing is eliminated since recall is required.
3. Mastery of greater amount of content can be measured because of reduced test time.

DISADVANTAGES OF COMPLETION TESTS
1. Do not measure higher levels of learning.
2. May have more than one defensible correct answer.

DISADVANTAGES OF COMPLETION TESTS FOR CBT

The disadvantages for CBT are the same as for essay tests with respect to including all possible variations of the answer and spelling tolerance (although not to the magnitude as in essay tests).

Simulations/Role Play

Simulations come in varying degrees when applied to CBT. The lowest level consists of video scenarios designed to depict certain skills, after which the students answer objective questions about the scenario. At the top end, there are actual simulators (such as flight simulators) that duplicate, to a very high degree, the actual conditions of performance but provide the element of safety if the task is dangerous. You want students to practice the skills involved in flying an aircraft before putting them in the cockpit.

Simulators involve the use of a complex computer programs that are highly interactive, can make subtle distinctions, and provide simulated feedback that approximates what would actually happen.

ADVANTAGES OF SIMULATIONS/ROLE PLAYS
1. Can depict subtleties of behavior that students must be aware of.
2. Create true problem solving situations for students to respond to.
3. Can evaluate complex skills.
4. Provide a model of behavior or performance for students to follow.

DISADVANTAGES OF SIMULATIONS/ROLE PLAYS
1. True simulators are very expensive to develop.
2. Unless involving true simulators, do not discriminate that students actually know how to perform complex skills, only that they recognize the components.
3. Unless true simulators, do not permit students to demonstrate the required mechanical skills.

Performance Tests

When true simulators are not feasible, an offline performance test is the best way to measure the skill level of students.

ADVANTAGES OF PERFORMANCE TESTS
1. The testing situation closely resembles actual work demands.
2. Measures skill proficiency very easily.
3. Trainees and evaluation report readers accept performance tests as valid measures because they directly measure realistic behavior.
4. Attained knowledge is assumed if students can perform to standards.

DISADVANTAGES OF PERFORMANCE TESTS
1. Must be carefully constructed to measure the end product, not the steps, unless there is a specified or preferred manner of performing the task.
2. Must go offline from the computer, which requires having a course administrator or other person, who is an expert in the field (also properly trained in administering and scoring the performance test), to make accurate observations.
3. Must retrain observers on a regular basis to ensure consistency among raters. This involves making video tapes and periodically collecting raters in a central location to establish consistency or by sending tapes to all locations, having raters rate the scenarios independently, and return to a central location for scoring. (For more information, see Chapter 5-3, the section on interater agreement.)
4. Costly to develop, administer, and score.
5. Financial and time constraints may make them impractical.

Capturing Test Data

Capturing responses to students' answers is a very important consideration. CBT allows for the storage of large quantities of student data for analysis. You must decide at this point during the design of the course the types of questions on which you want to capture data.

Table 3-8-1 in the Application Tools section of this chapter covers the various types of questions with respect to placement in a CBT course. If you want to conduct item analysis and distractor analysis on all types of questions, your authoring system must be built to capture that data. If you only want to capture data on quizzes and tests, that still must be build in.

We recommend that you capture as much information as possible on questions, at least through the pilot test. This data capturing mechanism is something that can be turned off at any time. If there is no need for it, turn it off after the pilot test to save storage space on the computer system's hard drive[12]. If there will be follow-on summative evaluation by you or the customer, leave the capability turned on until all summative evaluation is complete.

---

[12]If this capability is not shut off in those instances where it is not needed, it will continue to collect unneeded data until the amount of this data causes the system to crash because the hard drive can no longer accommodate it.

How To Do It

Constructing Essay Questions

Follow these guidelines when constructing an essay test:

1. Clearly fix the level that you want to write the question to and use appropriate verbs (i.e., compare, contrast, give reasons for, give original examples for) in the question.
2. Explain the overall task in the information that precedes the test.
3. Be certain that the task involved in completing the question is clearly defined.
4. Ask for supporting evidence for the student's answer.
5. To ensure test validity, have students complete the same questions rather than choose from a number of questions.
6. When you write essay questions for any type of delivery — paper-and-pencil, CBT — you must develop the scoring criteria ahead of time. What key words are you looking for in students' answers?
7. Establish a reasonable length for the question, in pages and in length of time, for students to compose the answer. Restricted essays actually require students to better compose their thoughts.
8. Use essay questions for those objectives that cannot be measured adequately through objective questions.

Following these criteria makes scoring essays much more objective because, no matter how much extraneous information is contained in the answer, you can focus on the essential elements and not get bogged down in the efforts of some students who write volumes in order to disguise lack of knowledge, hoping that you will not read the essay very closely. You should assign a certain number of points, depending on the importance of the essential points, and score the students' answers in relation to the completeness.

For example, in an essay on management skills, you might pose the following question:

"An employee has reported an incident of sexual harassment against another employee who reports to you. How would you handle this problem? Be certain to explain company policy regarding various consequences, data gathering information, and counseling the employee. Compose your answer using no more than three pages. You should spend no more than 30 minutes on this question." (50 points)

The criteria you should establish for students answers might include:

How well does the student explain company policy through his or her handling of the situation: before discussing the issue with the employee, during the discussion with the employee, and after discussion with the employee?

a. Does the student systematically gather information about the incident? (10 points)
b. Does the student fully explain, and interpret accurately, company policy and the possible consequences to the employee? (20 points)
c. Does the student view the topic from both positions, raise objections that the employee might raise, and handle those objections? (20 points)

Constructing Multiple Choice Questions

Multiple Choice test items should be constructed using the following guidelines:

1. The question stem should contain a verb.
2. The stem must clearly formulate a problem.
3. The stem should contain no extraneous information.
4. Make interrogatory stems complete sentences punctuated with a question mark.
5. Choices should contain clearly one correct answer.
6. Specify in the instructions if the student is to select the single correct, *or* the most correct, answer.
7. Don't use the following words:
   - always
   - never
   - simply
   - all of the above
   - none of the above
   - a combination of correct answers:
        Example: "Both A and C."
8. Have between 3 and 5 choices per question — one correct answer and three to four distractors; this avoids guessing. However, if the question does not lend itself to this many distractors, do not add obviously incorrect answers just to equalize all questions.
9. Increase the similarity between the possible answers to increase the difficulty of the questions.
10. Precede choices with an uppercase letter, A, B, C, D, E, to aid selection.
11. Incorporate video and/or graphics.
       Example: selecting three of four parts that are hot boxed on a video still.

Constructing Matching Questions

Consider the following guidelines when developing matching questions:
1. Have more possible answers than terms.
2. Provide instructions that are clear and concise in specifying how to match the stimulus to the response.
3. Co-locate stimuli and responses on one screen.
4. Identify stimuli by Arabic numbers (1, 2, etc.).
5. Have only one correct response for each stimuli.

6. Identify responses with uppercase letters commencing with A.
7. Make the ratio of responses to stimuli 3:2.
8. Place the stimuli column left of center with the responses column right of center.
9. Keep the lists of terms homogeneous.
10. Title the lists of terms and answers. (No, don't use the titles "Terms" and "Answers." Devise a short title that conveys the concept.)
11. Form answers using longer phrases than the terms.
12. Explain the basis for matching stimuli with responses and whether options can be used more than once.
13. Avoid repetitions of options in measuring associations.

Constructing True/False Questions

Use the following guidelines for constructing true/false questions:

1. Make items definitely true or definitely false without requiring additional qualifiers.
2. Use short stems that eliminate unnecessary material.
3. Keep statements approximately the same length whether they are true or false.
4. If opinion is used, attribute it to some source.
5. Be certain that there are equal numbers of true and false statements.
6. Avoid using double negative statements.
7. Randomize the questions after they are all written so that no pattern can develop — either intentionally or unintentionally.
8. The method of responding should be explained at the beginning of the test.
9. Always write questions in pairs.

Constructing Completion (Short Answer) Questions

There are two basic styles for short answer questions:

A. Require a word or phrase that completes a statement.
B. Require a definition, term defined, or computational formula.

Whichever type you chose to use, follow these guidelines when developing questions:

1. Make wording clear and comprehensive enough to allow the student who is knowledgeable to answer correctly.
2. Make the missing segment of the incomplete statement important, such as a key element of equipment.
3. Don't omit so many words as to make the statement unclear.
4. Specify the degree of accuracy of the answer and the units for computational problems.
5. Put the completion portion for incomplete statements at the end.

6. Use direct questions to test for comprehension of technical terms or knowledge of definitions.
7. Omit only consecutive key words.

Constructing Simulations/Role Plays

Use the following guidelines when constructing role plays:

1. Be sure to show positive examples of the situation you are depicting and have students evaluate it. (Show non-examples only of common errors.)
2. Use for guided practice.
3. Make relevant choices of the type of questions to ask and follow the prescribed guidelines to construct objective questions using the criteria above.

Constructing Performance Tests

Use the following guidelines when developing performance tests:

1. Analyze the work requirements by observing persons who are highly skilled at performing the task.
2. Provide practice of the task before evaluation.
3. Evaluate only the end result unless there is a specified or preferred way to achieve the end result.
4. Share the performance criteria with the student.

RATIONALE

Testing is the measure of the effectiveness of training. For formative evaluation, questions are included to identify any parts of a training course that may be ineffective. For summative evaluation, you must measure student improvement. For purposes of interactivity, you need to keep students involved and at the same time evaluate their learning and correct any errors immediately.

Choosing the right test to measure what the training was developed for is paramount to achieving usable results. You cannot test the performance of a person who has to complete complex mechanical tasks by administering a paper-and-pencil test. That would be like having an automobile mechanic demonstrate that he or she can tear down and reassemble an engine by giving him or her an essay test. The reverse is true if the CBT course teaches writing; the skills cannot be measured on a matching or true/false test.

While knowledge is the beginning of knowing how to do something, when we stop short of measuring how well they can actually perform the task, we have left 80% undone. **There is a vast difference between knowing 'about' something and actually knowing 'how to do' something.**

APPLICATION TOOLS

You must have consistent evaluation points to check for student understanding and track progress. Table 3-8-1 lists three types of questions, the taxonomic level, purpose, and recommended frequency of use in CBT courseware.

Figure 3-8-1 is a checklist for your test questions. When you can check off each of the criteria for correctly constructed questions, they are ready to put together for a test.

The testing plan in Chapter 5-3 and the Detailed Content Outline are the other Application Tools for this chapter.

Table 3-8-1
Question Types

Type	Location	Level	Purpose	Frequency
Embedded	Within a lesson.	Basic knowledge and understanding.	For basic motivation and interaction; tests knowledge of a step within a topic being covered.	Interspersed throughout a lesson.
Quiz	At the end of each lesson.	Knowledge of information within a lesson.	Test students' grasp of concepts within a lesson. (Questions should assume the knowledge from previous lessons and concentrate on information from current lesson only.) NOTE: Questions should test only the major concepts from the objective(s) that the lesson covers.	End of a lesson. NOTE: At least one question should be asked on each major topic or Lesson Objective (LO).
Test	Interim and End of Course	Application	Testing students' knowledge or performance by integrating information from throughout the course.	As required. NOTE: Test pool will contain at least one question from each Terminal Objective (TO).

Figure 3-8-1
Question Checklist

If all of the items listed can be checked, the question/overall test meets the criteria for inclusion in the CBT course.

____ The item measures the knowledge/behavior required by the objective.

____ The item is clearly supported by text.

____ The stem of the item states a central problem.

____ The item can stand alone out of context.

____ The item is clear, brief, and direct.

____ All distractors are plausible.

____ All distractors are approximately the same length.

____ Options are parallel in category, structure, and length.

____ Options are grammatically consistent with the stem.

____ There is clearly only one correct answer.

____ The choice of words does not give away the correct answer.

____ Key words (most, best, least, not) are underlined.

____ The item is free of poor logic.

____ The item is free of sexism.

____ Superfluous words, phrases, or sentences that do not contribute to the meaning of the item are absent.

____ Such words as "always" or "never" are omitted from options as they are generally false and put the student on alert.

____ Ambiguous words are omitted that can trick, mislead, or confuse a student into choosing the incorrect answer.

____ No verbatim excerpts from text are included. Items are paraphrased or presented in the working language of the job so that the students will grasp the principle rather than merely recognize a word or phrase.

____ Never use catch-all options (all of the above, none of the above).

____ Negative items (not, except) are used sparingly.

____ Options such as "both a and c" and "neither a nor b" are never used.

Unit 3 References

> **These are specific references for the chapters in this unit. For additional resources on topics in this unit, see the Bibliography.**

Chapter 3-1

Dick, W. & Carey, L. (1990). *The Systematic Design of Instruction.* Third Edition. Glenview, IL: Scott, Foresman.

Chapter 3-2

Merrill, M. D. (1983). Component Display Theory. In C. Reigeluth, Editor, *Instructional Design Theories and Models.* Hillsdale, NJ: Lawrence Erlbaum.

Chapter 3-7

Aldridge, H. & Liggett, L. (1990). *Audio/Video Production: Theory and Practice.* Englewood Cliffs, NJ: Prentice Hall.

Chapter 3-8

Kubiszyn, T. & Borich, G. (1987). *Educational Testing and Measurement: Classroom Application and Practice.* Glenview, IL: Scott, Foresman.

Merrell, A. (1993). Ten Evaluation Instruments for Technical Training. *Technical and Skills Training,* 4(5), pp. 7–14.

UNIT 4

Development

Doug is shown here integrating the video, audio, graphics, and text in a CBT lesson during Post Production using the authoring station.

INTRODUCTION

In the Development Phase, storyboards become programmed lessons. Easy to say, but more complex in execution. The responsibility is placed in the hands of people who have to be counted on to do their jobs well and deliver each piece on time. This can be cause for some feelings of insecurity. Team meetings are extremely important during the Development Phase to coordinate all of the various activities that are taking place.

UNIT CONTENT

The Development Phase consists of three major parts: Pre-production, Production, and Post Production. We also include a chapter on the Implementation Phase — the more hardware-intensive phase of the ISD Process — with respect to the instructional support that you need. (This Unit assumes the existence of a complete CBT project, using the full range of multimedia support available at the present time. It is possible, of course, not to use, e.g., video-based sequences produced especially for a specific project, and to go with a lower-budget approach, depending on the specifics of the situation, the environment, the group involved, and numerous other individual factors.) The four topics that make up this unit are:

1. **Pre-production**
   > What occurs at the Pre-production meeting
   > Who is in charge
   > Who is involved
   > The outcome of the Pre-production meeting

2. **Production**
   > Software Development Systems
   > Electronic Performance Support Systems
   > Video
   > Audio
   > Graphics/Text
   > Authoring

3. **Post Production**
   > Integration of video, audio, graphics, text
   > Review cycles – Functional Review

4. **Implementation Advice**
   > Technical Support
   > Machine Configuration
   > Software Configuration

CHAPTER 4-1
PRE-PRODUCTION

INTRODUCTION

Pre-production involves a meeting to review storyboards and make final determinations about what goes into the actual production of the various aspects of the CBT before each of the groups involved begin work.

There are a number of team members that must be included in the pre-production meeting.

1. The Instructional Designer (ID) who storyboarded the lesson.
2. The Author (Programmer) assigned to program the lesson.
3. The Audio Specialist who will record the audio.
4. The Video Specialist (Director) who will coordinate the video production.
5. The Subject Matter Expert (SME) for the lesson.
6. A representative from Standards.

WHAT TO DO

Instructional Designer

The ID is responsible for organizing and conducting the pre-production meeting. He or she must duplicate the storyboards that will be finalized during the meeting and distribute a copy to each of the team members who will attend.

The storyboards should be distributed well in advance of the meeting — we recommend a minimum of two days, but more time is better! Distribution time of a few hours is not acceptable because each pre-production team member has the responsibility to thoroughly review the storyboards and bring questions, comments, and suggestions to the meeting. When storyboards are distributed, the time, place, and date of the pre-production meeting should be announced.

The ID also leads the meeting, asks for questions and suggestions, and clarifies instructional design issues.

Author (Programmer)

The Author reviews the storyboards and comes to the meeting prepared to ask for clarification and makes suggestions regarding the programming of the lesson.

Audio Specialist

The audio specialist reviews the storyboards and comes to the meeting prepared to ask for clarification and make suggestions regarding the audio that is written for the lesson.

Video Specialist (Director)

The video specialist reviews the storyboards and comes to the meeting prepared to ask for clarification on the video shots (angles, content, special video effects, etc.)

Subject Matter Expert

The SME comes to the meeting prepared to give technical advice and make certain that any changes to the storyboards do not create technical errors in the lesson.

Standards

The representatives from Standards attends the meeting to determine that changes made during the meeting conform to the Course Design Specifications (CDS).

How To Do It

Conducting the Pre-production Meeting

At the pre-production meeting, each person, in turn, raises questions, requests clarification or changes, and makes suggestions about aspects of the storyboard that comes within their area of specialization.

This meeting is the forum at which to resolve conflicts, negotiate differences, and achieve consensus about all aspects of the lesson before moving ahead to production. While some restraints must be imposed for reasons of logistics or constraints imposed by the platform used for authoring, you want to be careful not to stifle the creativity of the lesson design.

Keep the emphasis on the fact that "only the project wins." We like to use the analogy of an orchestra when the subject of creativity arises. The members of the orchestra did not write the music so would you say that they are not creative? We wouldn't agree that the orchestra members are not creative unless each member of the orchestra decided to interpret the music in their own way and decide to play in the key of their own choice. The CDS (personified by the Standards representative) is the "conductor" who actually interprets.

Final Authority Vested in Standards Representative

The Standards representative has one additional responsibility at the meeting. If an issue reaches an impasse and discussion continues for too long without a foreseeable solution, the Standards representative can stop the discussion and make a final decision **that cannot be questioned**. The Standards representative's decision can be based on the best information from the various positions presented or it can be a completely different idea of their own preference as long as the solution conforms to the CDS. The fact that the decision cannot be questioned is very important for two reasons:

1. It puts teams on notice that they had best be able to come to agreement if they want to maintain control of the decision.

2. It prevents an impasse from stopping the pre-production meeting — an impasse that would ultimately delay the production schedule.

RATIONALE

"The Show Must Go On" to put it in theatrical terms. All issues must be resolved during the pre-production meeting so that all of the team members can go off on their own and complete the tasks of forming those individual aspects that will eventually become the lessons that roll up into the CBT course.

APPLICATION TOOLS

The storyboard is the only application tool for Pre-production.

CHAPTER 4-2
PRODUCTION

INTRODUCTION

The finalized storyboards are known as Production Baseline Storyboards. At this point each person or group understands what is required to produce the lesson; thus, the individual parts for the CBT lesson can be produced. Each part seems to be forming in isolation but the storyboard is the guiding factor that cements the parts together.

The authors know exactly what they will get from the video team, the audio team, the graphics team, and where each of their contributed components goes. When everyone does their job efficiently and effectively (which the storyboard allows them to do), much of the mystery is removed about how a seemingly chaotic effort becomes a "thing of beauty" that is also instructionally sound.

WHAT TO DO

Software Development Systems

There are a multitude of software packages available for integrating all of the production elements. These range from complete authoring systems to the various computer languages. Bergman and Moore (1990) list six "authoring facilities." General programming languages (such as Basic or C+) were not originally developed for adaptation to CBT development. However, they can be used for low-end CBT courseware. They require entering variable strings of alphanumeric code. Lines of code can become quite extensive and one misplaced period, comma, or other encoded information can require hours of debugging. Most authoring systems are based on these general languages but the language is encoded into the system and the bugs are already worked out.

Low End/High End Authoring Systems

Authoring facilities were developed specifically to support CBT. These facilities can be, at the low end, as simple as to permit only text to be displayed on the screen or as complex, at the high end, as authoring systems that contain the entire structure of a course and even provide prompts as to the type of information that needs to be typed into the system. The system then takes the information and converts it to a CBT lesson complete with full multimedia integration.

Most new authoring systems coming to market today are "icon based," which means that there are certain pre-programmed variable strings already resident in the authoring system (or special ones designed for unique functions can be developed by the author). The author can choose (click on) any one of these icons depending upon the function he or she wants to insert into the course at a certain point. Icons can be developed for such functions as questions screens. Icons can have variations to accommodate different types of questions (multiple choice, true/false, etc.). A survey by *CBT Solutions* (1993) revealed the most commonly recognized authoring systems. They are listed in Appendix B. We also recommend Milheim's (1994) book on authoring-systems software.

You should choose the authoring language or system based on the requirements of the training. Simple courses with some branching, text, graphics, and animation, can be accommodated with low end authoring systems that can be delivered from a floppy disk at any computer with minimal requirements for memory. Courses that require complex branching and multimedia integration mandate high end authoring systems. High end systems also require many more hardware requirements (disc players, CD ROM, memory storage) for development and for delivery. The more requirements, the more expensive.

> NOTE: Most authoring software comes with training included as part of the package price or as an option. Take the training! Send your authors for training well in advance of the Design Phase. Authors must know the capabilities of the system before anyone can design the user interface.

CBT vs. EPSS

CBT is usually defined as containing the elements of instruction outlined in the unit on Design. CBT will contain an introduction, present content in the form of instruction, provide practice, test, etc. Electronic Performance Support Systems (EPSS), on the other hand, are usually considered as job aids to assist a worker in performing some task. The performance of the task can be online or offline.

An example of an online EPSS is a system for filling out purchases orders in a warehouse. The EPSS will prompt the user to fill in certain areas at certain times, in a certain sequence. When the sequence is completed, the result is an actual purchase order.

An example of an offline EPSS is a system that can troubleshoot and diagnose problems in a sophisticated piece of electronic equipment. The repair person will enter certain information into a computer in response to prompts that query the symptoms of the problem. The computer will sort through its files and narrow the possible problems. The repair person can then go through the possible problems provided until correct diagnosis is made. Once diagnosed by the computer, the machine is repaired by the person, not the computer.

CBT/EPSS Integration

Users of EPSS must usually be trained to operate the support system. This training can be accomplished in the classroom or on the job. Increasingly, however, the EPSS has a component of CBT included.

True integration of CBT and EPSS is now possible by having the training and the support system "cross over" or become "integrated."

Backing Up CBT Files

Before we talk about any type of production, we would be remiss in not telling you about backing up your computer files. Either work on your hard disk and back up to floppy, or vice versa. Most computers have an automatic backup that you can set through the program management function menu. Set this to backup frequently, at least every five minutes for detailed work. Automatic backup sends your files periodically to another file on the hard drive. But each day also back your files up onto a floppy disk and store them separately.

Hard disks "crash" — break down — and you can lose significant amounts of work. Don't have to learn this the hard way, like we did. Take our advice and make backup copies of your work at these intervals suggested, or more often — but not less often.

With this background information we can move on to our discussion of Production Teams. Each of the teams performs its part as outlined in the following sections.

Authors (Programmers)

Programmers begin to type the graphic text and put together the framework for the lesson to which they can later add the video, graphics, and audio, according to the CDS and Programmer's Guide established during the Design Phase.

Graphics

Graphic artists create the graphics and animation sequences, log them, and store them according to the file naming conventions that were established in the CDS and Programmer's Guide and which meet the file naming requirements of your authoring system.

Video

Video creates shot lists, shoots the video sequences, and logs them according to the Course Design Specifications.

Video Team

The video team is generally the largest in terms of numbers of people. The video team usually consists of the producer, the director, the camera operators, lighting and sound experts, set designers and decorators, and costume designers, assuming that your organization has opted for high end, multimedia CBT.

Director

Normally, in video, it is the Producer's job to assemble the rest of the video team but we have found that this is better left to the Director, who has specialized knowledge about video. The Director is responsible for recruiting, auditioning, and choosing the actors who will perform in the video. The Director will know of local talent agencies who will send photos, resumes, and whatever else is needed to choose the talent who will audition. The Director must rehearse the on-screen talent, and supervise set construction, set decoration crews, and camera operators. Overall, the Director's job is to be certain that everything runs smoothly from either the set or the control room.

NOTE: For large productions you might have a producer who is charge of arranging the entire shoot and an assistant director who works with the director when the director needs to be two places at once. In video shoots, these two positions are usually combined with the director's position. On most video shoots there is an assistant who is used by the director as a "gopher" — "*go for* cables"; "*go for* sandwiches." However, if your budget can afford them or it is a "really big shoot," it is best to have three individuals — one for each position.

Set Designers/Builders

Set Designers are those persons who determine what the set will look like and those on the construction crew who build any backdrops required for the video shoot.

Set Decorators

Set Decorators are those persons who will gather props and set the scene according to the instructions of the Producer.

Wardrobe

Wardrobe must find or make the clothing that is worn by the on-screen talent, if they cannot supply it themselves.

Camera Crew

The camera crew are those persons who will do the actual filming or videotaping to capture the scene.

On-Screen Talent

The actors who must memorize scripts and rehearse. Narrators generally fall under this category, although their cost will vary from that of actors.

Lighting

The lighting crew must carefully set the lights to accent the scene.

Sound

Sound experts set the microphones to achieve the best audio reproduction and also run the recording equipment, whether in a studio setting from the control room or on location.

Instructional Designer

The ID as technical advisor should be on the set to help establish the shots according to the storyboard so that the concept can be depicted the way it was intended. The ID will also review final footage and help choose the shots to use. Other than that, the Director is in charge.

Subject Matter Expert

The SME can be on the video set or on call for final details on the technical aspects of the lesson and to make certain that the scene is technically correct. The SME is also involved in the review of final footage with the ID to choose which shots to use in the lesson.

How To Do It

Video Shoots and Shot Lists

As the video is shot, use the Shot List in the Application Tools section of this chapter (see Figure 4-2-1) to identify each sequence shot. Shoot each sequence several times from the preferred angle designated on the storyboard and from a couple of different angles just in case the desired shot does not work out as well as it was conceived. You want to prevent as many reshoots as possible for two reasons:

1. Because they are expensive — you have to reassemble:
   - talent
   - crew
   - sets
   - costumes
   - make sure that, if the scene is in sequence, that everything is the same (actor's hair, clothing, props).
2. Because sometimes they are impossible to reconstruct: the same problems occur in reassembling the required people and elements as in number 1.

Fill in the following elements on the Shot List:

1.	Shot Number	Sequentially numbered shots for the lesson.
2.	Storyboard Number	The storyboard sequence where the shot will be used.

3.   Brief Description   Two or three words that will convey the essence of the shot.

4.   File Name   To be filled in with the file convention name from the CDS.

5.   Used/Reshot   To be filled in after the disk is logged in Post Production to determine if the shot was used. If reshot, the number of the new shot should be indicated here and the reshoot number listed at the bottom of the Shot List.

6.   Disposition   *Buy* – this is the shot chosen for use in the course.
OK – this shot can be used if there are no better ones available.
NG – "no good," this shot has errors and cannot be used.

7.   Logged   The camera has a running meter that can tell where a shot began (IN) and where it ended (OUT).

Elements 1 through 4 are filled in during the shoot by the Director's assistant. Elements 5 through 7 are completed during review and logging in Post Production.

Audio Recording and Logging

As audio is recorded, use the Audio Log in the Application Tools section (Figure 4-2-2) to keep track of each audio segment. Be sure to fill in each of the following sections on the log:

1.   Number   Sequentially numbered audio segments for the lesson.

2.   Storyboard Number   The storyboard sequence where the audio will be used.

3.   Brief Description   Two or three words that will convey the essence of the audio.

4.   File Name   To be filled in with the file convention name from the CDS.

5.   Used/Re-recorded   This section will be filled by the ID and SME when they determine which audio will be used. If re-recorded, the number of the new audio should be indicated here and the new number listed at the bottom of the Audio Log as a cross-reference.

6.	Disposition of Bite	*Buy* – this is the bite chosen for use in the course.
		OK – this bite can be used if there are no better ones available.
		NG – "no good," this bite has errors and cannot be used.
7.	Logged	The audio recorder in the sound studio has a running meter that can tell where a segment began (IN) and where it ended (OUT).

Elements 1 through 4 are filled in during recording by the sound expert. Elements 5 through 7 are completed during review and logging in Post Production.

Drawing and Logging Graphics

The graphic artist draws the graphics and animation sequences on the computer and saves them to a floppy disk. The artist must log the graphic using the Graphics Log (Figure 4-2-4). Fill in these elements of the Graphics Log:

1.	Number	Sequentially numbered graphic segments for the lesson.
2.	Storyboard Number	The storyboard sequence where the graphic will be used.
3.	File Name	To be filled in with the file convention name from the CDS or Programmer's Guide. Each frame in an animation must be logged separately but identified as part of a sequence.
4.	Brief Description	Two or three words that will describe the graphic.

Graphics must be viewed in association with any audio that describes it to be certain that the two match. This is best done during Post Production when the two are integrated. You must be sure that there is enough pause between graphic builds and that there is sufficient audio during the length of time the graphic is on the screen.

Requesting Graphics Rework

There are four instances when requests for graphics rework may be called for:

1. Depiction is unclear (i.e., cannot clearly see what is being discussed, too small, colors of adjacent items interfere, undefined borders between important areas).
2. The proportions are incorrect.
3. Animation sequencing is incorrect (step out of sequence, or totally off).
4. Incorrect standards are applied (font size, style, color, etc.).

If graphics need rework, user the Graphic Rework Request (Figure 4-2-7).

Reviewing Audio and Video

Each team completes its individual portion of the storyboard. Then the ID and the SME review the video and the audio to be certain that they look and sound the way they are intended. Follow along on the finalized storyboard to check these two elements.

If there is no video that can be used from all the takes, use the Reshoot Request Form (Figure 4-2-5) to request a reshoot. Fill in each section completely so that the Director clearly understands the problem with the old shot and the set up of the new shot. Of course, the ID and SME should be on the set for all reshoots, just as they were for the original shots.

The video must be viewed in association with any audio that describes it to be certain that they match. However, this is done during Post Production when the two are integrated. You must be sure that there is enough pause between screen builds and that there is sufficient audio during the length of time the video is running.

Requesting Reshoots and Re-records

Reshoots may be required for three reasons:

1. None of the takes available clearly indicate or show what is required to teach the concept.
2. There is a change to the system (i.e., machine) that is being shown.
3. There is an error in the video or contradiction between the video and audio.

Let us reemphasize again that reshoots translate into big money in video because of the difficulty, and sometimes impossibility, of reassembling all of the people and elements required to reshoot one scene or segment of a scene. Careful planning, using the SME and ID on the set, and multiple takes the first time, are much less costly.

Requests for re-recording audio can be for two reasons:

1. The audio is incorrect (e.g., a word mispronounced, wrong inflection, etc.)
2. The audio needs to be changed (e.g., due to a change in the machine you are describing).

If the audio requires a re-record because of the first circumstance, use the Audio Review and Error List (Figure 4-2-3). If the requirement is a complete re-record, use the Re-record Request Form (Figure 4-2-6).

All reviews and logging must be done very carefully because the next step is to transfer the video and audio to tape and ship it to be mastered. Any errors discovered on the check disk will create a delay in the schedule and cost money while the disk is returned for remastering.

RATIONALE

CBT production, and especially high end multimedia CBT, is a very complex procedure and is the one aspect of development that is in the hands of the largest number of people all working, seemingly, in total isolation. But that's far from the truth in a well orchestrated project. It is, however, the one place where the greatest number of problems can occur in an unorganized project.

There is no magic to CBT when it all comes together. The success is the result of a well organized project where everyone knows what needs to be done and does it in a coordinated manner so that everything can be fed to the author at the specified time in the schedule. Success can also be the result of a lot of hair pulling and frustration if all elements are not coordinated. How would you rather work?

APPLICATION TOOLS

The tools provided here are:

1. Shot List
2. Audio Log
3. Audio Review and Error List
4. Graphics Log
5. Reshoot Request
6. Re-record Request
7. Graphic Rework Request

Figure 4-2-1
Shot List

Lesson Number _____
Unit Number _____
Lesson Title _____

Director _____
Logged by _____
Date Logged _____

Shot Number	Storyboard Number	Brief Description	File Name	Used/Reshot (Reshoot No.)	Disposition	Logged IN	Logged OUT

Shot List Key

Shot Number	Sequentially numbered shots for the lesson.
Storyboard Number	The storyboard sequence where the shot will be used.
Brief Description	Two or three words that will convey the essence of the shot.
File Name	To be filled in with the file convention name from the CDS or Programmer's Guide.
Used/Reshot	Will be filled in after the disk is logged in Post Production to determine if the shot was used. If reshot, the number of the new shot should be indicated here and the reshoot number listed on the next blank line at the bottom of the Shot List.
Disposition	*Buy* — this is the shot chosen for use in the course. *OK* — this shot can be used if there are no better ones available. *NG* — "no good," this shot has errors and cannot be used.
Logged	The camera has a running meter that can tell where a shot began (IN) and where it ended (OUT).

NOTE: The first four elements are filled in during the shoot by the director's assistant. The last three are completed during review and logging in Post Production.

Figure 4-2-2
Audio Log

Lesson Number _____
Unit Number _____
Lesson Title _____

Sound Director _____
Logged by _____
Date Logged _____

Segment Number	Storyboard Number	Brief Description	File Name	Used/Re-recorded (Re-record. No.)	Disposition	Logged IN	Logged OUT

Audio Log Key

Number	Sequentially numbered audio segments for the lesson.
Storyboard Number	The storyboard sequence where the audio will be used.
Brief Description	Two or three words that will convey the essence of the audio.
File Name	To be filled in with the file convention name from the CDS.
Used/ Re-recorded	Will be filled in after the disk is logged in Post Production to determine if the audio was used. If re-recorded, the number of the new audio file should be indicated here and the new number listed on the next blank line at the bottom of the Audio Log as a cross-reference.
Disposition	*Buy* – this is the bite chosen for use in the course. *OK* – this bite can be used if there are no better ones available. *NG* – "no good," this bite has errors and cannot be used.
Logged	The audio recorder in the sound studio has a running meter that can tell where a segment began (IN) and where it ended (OUT).

NOTE: The first four elements are filled in during recording by the sound expert. The last three elements are completed during review and logging in Post Production.

Figure 4-2-3
Audio Review and Error List

Record any errors in the audio on this sheet and return it to the audio production team for re-recording.

Requester _____
Lesson Number _____
Unit Number _____
Lesson Title _____

Date _____
Sound Director _____
Logged by _____

Segment Number	Storyboard Number	Description of Error	File Name	Original Segment		New Segment		Date Logged
				IN	OUT	IN	OUT	

IMPORTANT NOTE: Be sure to record the audio file changes on the master audio record list.

Audio Review and Error List Key

Segment Number	Running list of the number of segments where errors occur.
Storyboard Number	The storyboard identification page where the error was found so that the narrator can quickly identify where the segment is that needs to be re-recorded.
Brief Description	A description of the error identified.
File Name	The audio file name.
Old Segment	The beginning (IN) and end (OUT) of the original audio segment.
New Segment	The beginning (IN) and end (OUT) of the new audio segment.
Date Logged	Date the new audio segment was logged onto the master audio file list.

Figure 4-2-4
Graphics Log

Lesson Number _____
Unit Number _____
Lesson Title _____

Graphic Artist _____
Logged by _____
Date Logged _____

Graphic Number	Storyboard Number	File Name	Brief Description of Graphic

Graphics Log Key

Number — Sequentially numbered graphic segments for the lesson.

Storyboard Number — The storyboard sequence where the graphic will be used.

File Name — To be filled in with the file convention name from the CDS. Each frame in an animation sequence must be logged separately but identified as part of a sequence. (Animation sequences will be specified by the CDS but would normally be identified with an alphanumeric extension on the file name.)

Brief Description — Two or three words that will describe the graphic.

Figure 4-2-5
Reshoot Request

Requester _____   Date of Request _____

Unit Number _____   Old Shot Counter IN _____

Lesson Number _____   Old Shot Counter OUT _____

Lesson Title _____

Reason for Request

Explanation of New Shot Needed

Completed:

Date _____   By Whom _____
New Shot IN _____   New Shot OUT _____
Logged Date _____

Figure 4-2-6
Re-record Request

Requester _____   Date of Request _____

Unit Number _____   Old Segment Counter IN _____

Lesson Number _____   Old Segment Counter OUT _____

Lesson Title _____

Reason for Request

New Audio (Written as Needed)

Completed:

Date _____   By Whom _____

New Shot IN _____   New Shot OUT _____

Logged Date _____

Figure 4-2-7
Graphic Rework Request

Requester _____   Date of Request _____
Unit Number _____   File Number _____
Lesson Number _____   File Name _____

Lesson Title _____

Reason for Request

Explanation of New Graphic

Completed:
Date _____   By Whom _____
Graphic File Number _____ File Name _____
Logged Date _____

CHAPTER 4-3
POST PRODUCTION

Introduction

During Post Production, all of the segments of the lessons and units are brought together by the Author, and the final formative evaluation reviews of the courseware is conducted. These final reviews are coordinated through Configuration Control, as outlined in Unit 1.

Before that can happen, the audio and visual media must be configured and finalized. We recommend that you refer to Bergman and Moore's book (1990) for detailed information on mastering videodiscs and/or CD ROM.

What To Do

Preparing for Disk Mastering

The final video that has been chosen for the lesson is transferred to tape and sent to have the videodisc or CD ROM mastered. This "disk geography" requires that all of the video segments be placed on a master videotape in the order[13] they will be used and all of the audio is transferred to a final audio tape.

Mastering a Disk

Mastering involves transferring all of the video and audio to the delivery medium. You may have the internal capabilities to do this or you may need to send the audio and video to a technical facility that specializes in mastering disks. If reviews of audio and video were carefully done during Production, you should not have any errors in the video or audio.

Logging a Check Disk

It is extremely important that all of the video and audio is logged accurately so that the author can identify the exact point at which the audio and video begins and ends. The first disk that returns to you from the company that masters the disk is called a check disk. This disk must be reviewed for three reasons:

1. To be certain that all of the video is on the disk.
2. To be certain that all of the audio is on the disk.
3. That it is of high quality (free of video glitches, etc.).

Authoring

Authors have the major responsibility for integrating all of the video, audio, graphics, and graphic text into the shell they developed during Production.

---

[13] Shots don't have to be in order but ordering them according to the sequence they will be used in the course will make the program run faster, making for a more professional product.

Review Cycles

Conduct two of the review cycles that you conducted during the Design Phase:

- Standards Review
- Editorial Review

In addition to the above reviews, you need to conduct a Functional Review. The purpose of this review is to be certain that there are no bugs in the programming logic and no glitches in the audio, video, or graphics. A Functional Review Form (Figure 4-3-1) is included in the Application Tools section of this chapter.

You don't need an Instructional Review at this point. The instructional effectiveness of the course was determined by the review during the Design Phase. Nor do you need a Management Review; at this point the courseware should meet the requirements of the contract based on the review of the Storyboards during the Design Phase. A Technical Review is also unnecessary at this point. The SME has reviewed the technical accuracy of the storyboards, participated in the Pre-production meeting, been on the set for video shoots, and reviewed the final video and audio with the ID.

How To Do It

Logging Video and Audio

When the check disks return, both audio and video must be viewed and each video and audio segment must again be checked against the log for correct IN/OUT sequence, recording where the video and audio begin and end.

Review each video and audio segment on the development platform, noting any glitches (jumps) on the disk that sometimes occur during mastering. Once the disk is determined to be completely accurate, orders can be placed for the quantities of disks to be pressed.

When the final disk returns, the video and audio segments are recorded on the proper place on the Storyboard (Audio In, Audio Out on the Storyboard Template provided in Unit 3, Design) to identify where each frame of video and segment of audio appears on the disk.

It is good to review a sample number of the final disks in case one or more are bad. Obviously, you can't review every disk. Therefore, you may send one out that might have been damaged during pressing. Such things happen, although rarely. You should probably count on your customer contacting you about a certain number of bad disks so order a few extra to cover these occurrences. You want to get a disk back to the customer as soon as possible. If you have to send the damaged disk back to the mastering house and wait for a new one, your customer loses valuable time during which students are waiting to be trained.

Author

The Author uses the storyboard with the audio/video files listed as a reference to program the computer to pick up the correct segments and shots and run them at the correct spot in the lesson. The Author integrates all of the elements for the videodisc, CD ROM, and from the graphics files (now loaded on to the hard drive — sometimes called the hard card — in the machine) that have been created for each lesson.

Technical Support

The lessons must be loaded on correctly configured computers by technical support personnel in preparation for final review. The requirements of technical support are discussed in Chapter 4-4.

Review Cycles

Follow the same steps used during the Design Phase (see Chapter 3-6) to conduct the necessary reviews of the online lessons. After all reviews are completed and necessary changes recorded on the review forms, return the storyboard and review form to CC (see Chapter 1-5), who returns it to the Author for changes and reintegration. Reviews must contain enough detail so that the Author knows exactly what needs to be changed.

The numbers on the Online Lesson Review Forms (Figure 4-3-3) should coincide with a storyboard number (which now matches a screen number) and there should be a separate page for each storyboard. The first reviewer should number the Review Form pages. If more than one page is required for a screen of the lesson, subsequent pages should be numbered with an alpha character (i.e., 1, 1A, 1B, etc.). Blank copies of all the review forms (Editorial, Standards, Functional) should also be included in the packet of Online Lesson Review Forms. Each review form should be completed by the reviewer assigned for that purpose.

CC's responsibility is to list the lessons on the Review Scheduling Form as each set becomes available. It is the reviewers' responsibility to check the list on a regular basis to determine that lessons are ready for review. Should the Author remove the lesson from review at any time, it should be indicated on the schedule with the Author's name beside the appropriate time and day.

Each reviewer (Editorial, Standards, Functional) records errors on the same page. This helps the Author correct all errors on one screen at one time. This format speeds up the process over the Author having to review the comments of each reviewer on a separate page.

All reviewers should complete their reviews on the same machine. Scheduling the machine becomes an issue so that reviewers can plan their reviews. A Scheduling Form (see Figure 4-3-4) is supplied in the Application Tools section. The last reviewer to complete a review and sign the scheduling form should return the Online Lesson Review Forms to CC for return to the Author. Until the last review is completed, all review forms should remain with the configured machine.

After the Author corrects the identified changes, there is no need to have each reviewer go through the lesson again. One person should be assigned to validate that the changes have been made. A check mark beside each change validates the change has been reviewed and corrected.

RATIONALE

Post Production is another area that is in the hands of a large number of people (although fewer than during Production). It is also the first time the project leaves your hands (when sent for mastering). Whenever the project leaves you, there is always a certain amount of concern. Rest assured, however, that most mastering houses have high standards of quality control.

These efforts take a lot of coordination to make everything run smoothly. There are lessons to load on the computer, reviews to complete, changes to be made for the final delivery. You must maintain control over versions of software as corrections are completed so that the final, most correct, and highest quality software gets shipped to the customer.

APPLICATION TOOLS

Tools provided here are:

1. Functional Review Instructions. (Other Review Instructions are found in the Application Tools Section of the Unit on Design.)
2. Functional Review Form. (Other Review Instructions are found in the Application Tools Section of the Unit on Design.)
3. Online Lesson Review Form.
4. Review Scheduling Form.

Figure 4-3-1
Functional Review Directions

A functional review of online lessons and courses assures that the material is free of bugs and is of professional quality.

The Course Design Specification is the guide to establishing the standards for courseware design and development. The functional review determines if all of the functional aspects of the software execute correctly.

Review Procedures
Obtain a current copy of the lesson storyboards from Configuration Control. This should be the copy that the Author used to *execute* the lesson. Follow the storyboard closely to be sure that the functions to be checked operate in the manner that they were designed. Record any errors on the Online Lesson Review Form.

Functions
1. Function buttons must appear on each screen and work the way they are intended. Press each function button on each screen. Functions to check include:
   - Pause/Resume
   - Back
   - Replay
   - Continue
   - Hot Spots
   - All Main Menu Items (lists specific menu items on checklist)
   - Help Function
   - Quit Function
   - Others (list specifics on checklist)

Programming
1. Movement between screens is free of glitches, blips, or fatal errors that make the program crash.
2. Test the branching on each screen where there are options for the programming to go depending upon inputs. You will need to test each branching option by backing up to the original screen each time and choosing each possible option. If backing up is not possible from some screens, mark those areas; it will be necessary to go through the lesson again. Typical branching that must be checked are:
   - Embedded questions.
   - Quiz questions of a multiple choice format. Alternate between giving the correct answer first, then the incorrect answer first.
   - Expanded information based on incorrect student input. (These may be the most difficult branches to back out of since the lesson will typically move back to the main lesson after the information is delivered.)

3. Test the lesson using the longest path first (go through the lesson answering every question incorrectly and taking all remediation available). Then review the lesson again taking the shortest path (go though the lesson answering everything correctly).
4. Keep a tally of the number of questions answered correctly and incorrectly on questions that will be tracked and scored. Check this against the score given by the computer at the end of the lesson.
5. Be sure that the branching between lessons also functions smoothly, as intended.

Recording Errors
1. Record errors on the Online Lesson Review Form provided with each lesson.
2. Use the color assigned to record errors.
3. Be very specific in your description of the error.

Figure 4-3-2
Functional Review Form

Lesson Number _____

Date of Review _____

Lesson Name _____

Reviewer _____

Functions
___ Pause/Resume
___ Back
___ Replay
___ Continue
___ Hot Spots
___ All Main Menu Items (lists specific menu items here)

_____

_____

_____

_____

___ Help Function
___ Quit Function
___ Others (list specifics here)

_____

_____

_____

_____

Programming
___ Movement between screens is free of glitches, blips, and fatal errors.
___ Branching works correctly.
___ Embedded questions.
___ Quiz questions.
___ Expanded information.
___ Branching between lessons.
___ Quizzes and other scored items are recorded correctly.

Figure 4-3-3
Online Lesson Review Form

Lesson Number _____

Lesson Name _____   SB Number _____

Reviewer's Name _____   Date Completed _____

Editorial	Validated √

Reviewer's Name_____   Date Completed _____

Standards	Validated √

Reviewer's Name _____   Date Completed _____

Functional	Validated √

Changes Validated By: _____   Date Completed _____

Figure 4-3-4
Review Scheduling Form

Lesson Number and Title							
Reviewer's Name	Time	M	T	W	Th	F	Review Completed
	8:00						
	9:00						
	10:00						
	11:00						
	12:00						
	1:00						
	2:00						
	3:00						
	4:00						
	5:00						

CHAPTER 4-4
IMPLEMENTATION ADVICE

Introduction

Implementation involves the technical aspect of a CBT course to get it ready for delivery. Since the purely technical aspects of CBT are beyond the scope of this book, it doesn't get its own unit although it is a separate phase of the ISD Process. However, the technical requirements for successful delivery do warrant mention.

What To Do

The project team must have someone with technical support expertise to configure the authoring stations during development and the delivery systems during implementation. The technical support team members must have a high degree of knowledge and skill about the hardware platform on which your CBT courseware will be delivered. It is the responsibility of the technical support person to:

1. Coordinate the installation of the hardware for pilot studies and at implementation sites.
2. Coordinate the installation of software.
3. Maintain hardware and software during all testing and for the length of time required by the contract.
4. Be present at all times during the first pilot test and the initial testing of the software at implementation sites.
5. Troubleshoot problems that arise after initial installation.

Success of the pilot test, evaluation — indeed the overall success of the project — may depend on the skills of your technical support team. Even if your customer has a technical support team, your own group will probably have to do some initial work with the customer's team.

How To Do It

Use the Technical Support Checklist (Figure 4-4-1) in the Application Tools section of this chapter to be sure that the technical support person completes all tasks prior to implementation.

Rationale

Correctly configured machines make for smooth running of the training program. Thus, students can complete the training with few interruptions from hardware and software problems. A smoothly operating course makes for satisfied customers and repeat business. Many customers become discouraged with CBT and abandon future use because of a troublesome first attempt which was not actually the fault of the medium at all but a result of inadequate technical support.

APPLICATION TOOLS

Here is a checklist of considerations for the technical support you need prior to and during the evaluation of the CBT.

Figure 4-4-1
Technical Support Checklist

Complete all of the following activities for the implementation of the CBT program:

☐ Locate and set up all required hardware.

☐ Locate and install the correct version of all software.

☐ Test the hardware systems.

☐ Monitor the hardware and software during initial implementation.

☐ Troubleshoot hardware and software problems.

☐ Support customer's technical support team in their familiarization with the system and software.

Unit 4 References

> These are specific references for the chapters in this unit. For additional resources on topics in this unit, see the Bibliography.

Chapter 4-1

Bergman, R. & Moore, T. (1990). *Managing Interactive Video/Multimedia Projects.* Englewood Cliffs, NJ: Educational Technology Publications.

Chapter 4-2

Aldridge, H. & Liggett, L. (1990). *Audio/Video Production: Theory and Practice.* Englewood Cliffs, NJ: Prentice Hall.

Bergman, R. & Moore, T. (1990). *Managing Interactive Video/Multimedia Projects.* Englewood Cliffs, NJ: Educational Technology Publications.

Milheim, W. Editor. (1994). *Authoring-Systems Software for Computer-Based Training.* Englewood Cliffs, NJ: Educational Technology Publications.

Okonski, S. (November, 1993). The Future of Authoring Systems. *CBT Solutions.* Hingham, MA: SB Communications.

Chapter 4-3

Aldridge, H. & Liggett, L. (1990). *Audio/Video Production: Theory and Practice.* Englewood Cliffs, NJ: Prentice Hall.

Bergman, R. & Moore, T. (1990). *Managing Interactive Video/Multimedia Projects.* Englewood Cliffs, NJ: Educational Technology Publications.

Chapter 4-4

Bergman, R. & Moore, T. (1990). *Managing Interactive Video/Multimedia Projects.* Englewood Cliffs, NJ: Educational Technology Publications.

UNIT 5

Evaluation

Mike creates a comfortable and relaxed atmosphere as he conducts Ginger's interview after completing her CBT course. The information gathered through interviews should not be underestimated. However, it should not be the only type of information gathered.

INTRODUCTION

You just made your delivery date after many long hours and hard work; the product is now installed at your customer's site and it's being used. "What a relief" — for a few seconds. You are called in to your manager's office and given another assignment as a reward for a job well done. Actually what you need is a month off to recover from this project.

You really do have a certain satisfaction of a job well done. But if you ever had the time to reflect on what you had done, you might want to know if what you had developed was truly effective in teaching the students the skills needed to do the job for which the training was developed.

You have designed feedback to reinforce the learning of your students so that they can improve. Just as feedback keeps students on track, feedback on our design and effectiveness of the training helps us improve the next project.

But that requirement wasn't in the contract, and you're on to the next project, so you just put it in the back of your mind. We want to bring those thoughts to the foreground and have them nag at you a bit.

The fact is, however, that customers are becoming more and more sophisticated. Customers that we develop training for are asking for validation that the training is effective before they will accept or pay for it. The days are rapidly coming to an end when your team can abdicate responsibility for the effectiveness of the training. Groups that aren't willing to stand behind their products are telling customers that they don't have confidence in what they are doing.

Each chapter of Units 1 through 4 in this book has listed the formative evaluation procedures that must be conducted during each phase of the CBT development process. Let's review them:

1. Needs Assessment/Analysis is actually an evaluation function. You find out the customer's reason for requesting the project. His or her company or group in your company obviously has a problem. You need to find out what the problem is, how to correct the problem, and the methodology for delivering the solution (CBT, for the purposes of this book). You determined the readability requirements for the intended audience. Proving that the solution solves the problem is determined by summative evaluation (so the summative evaluation process actually begins during Assessment/Analysis).

2. During Design, you developed a training plan that included detailed instructional outlines and the tests for the training. Your team established the standards for the design and development. You established the content validity of the tests that will be used in the training. SMEs reviewed the design for the technical content accuracy; instructional experts reviewed the plan for instructional soundness. You validated the readability level of the course.

3. The Development Phase saw the creation of storyboards that went through review cycles to establish the adherence to technical and programming standards. You performed yet another series of reviews of the programmed lessons for technical and instructional purposes as well as adherence to programming standards. A functional review "debugged" the course.

4. During Implementation, you installed the training on your customers system and again checked the program for software or hardware "bugs." You completed a pilot study that saw members of the target audience complete the course and provide you with feedback. Changes were made to the CBT course based on the feedback.

If you have completed all of the tasks during the previous phases, formative evaluation is behind you. Now you are ready to judge the effectiveness of the training.

If you think that this treatment of Summative Evaluation is too academic, it's not. As a matter of fact, we have streamlined the process to the point that some researchers would probably wince. But we developed a system that works, violates no principles of research or statistical measurement, and that will yield the information you need in the shortest period of time—after all, in a deadline-driven environment, we don't have the luxury of extended research projects.

UNIT CONTENT

The chapters in this unit will cover the following:

1. **Purpose of Evaluation**
   Questions to ask
   How to get the answers
   Norm-Referenced Tests vs. Criterion-Referenced Tests
   Test Specifications
2. **Collecting Information**
   Dangers of Over Collecting or Under Collecting Data
   Surveys and Interviews
3. **Test Validity**
   Testing Plan
   Test Length
   Weighting Test Items
   Qualitative Measures
   Quantitative Measures
   Types of Validity
   Parallel Forms of Tests
4. **Using Appropriate Measures of Training's Effectiveness**
   Item Analysis
   Correlation
   Difficulty Index
5. **Testing Outcomes**
   Types of Tests Based on Desired Outcomes
6. **Legal and Ethical Issues**
   Equal Employment Opportunity Commission Guidelines
   Court Cases

CHAPTER 5-1
PURPOSE OF EVALUATION

INTRODUCTION

Evaluation is a decision-making process. We will cover the various questions that must be asked and, based on the answers, explain what you must do to accomplish the tasks required to get the information.

This chapter deals with making the decisions about the types of evaluation you need to conduct and then how to go about conducting them. The decisions you make must be based on what the CBT course is intended to do and how it will be used. While evaluation has not been a major consideration in many CBT projects in the past, that era has come to an end — you simply *must* devote considerable attention to it today.

WHAT TO EVALUATE

The matrix in Figure 5-1-1 shows the aspects of the decision-making process. The matrix shows the interrelation between the type and level of validity required by the purpose of the training. Note that the highest level of validation needed to satisfy the requirements of the purpose of the training is indicated with an X, but remember that *all levels of validity below the level indicated* are also required. Validation is a series of steps (that began with the formative evaluation steps already completed) that build to the level of validity required.

The first decision is whether the measurement variables are Organizational Goals or Employee Traits. If the variables are organizational goals, you will need to answer some or all of the following:

1. Is the customer getting a return on their investment (ROI) that justifies the amount of money that was spent on developing and implementing the CBT?

    To answer this question, you will have to collect data on the cost of the training the customer was delivering before the CBT was implemented and compare that information to data that you collect over a period of time after the CBT training is implemented. If there is no data available, you will have to collect as much information on the costs of presenting training while you are developing the CBT. From the information obtained before the new training was implemented, and for a period of several months after the CBT was installed, you can predict the effectiveness of the training over yet other extended periods of time to determine how long it will take for the CBT to pay for itself.

190

Figure 5-1-1
Validity Matrix

MEASUREMENT VARIABLE	PURPOSE	Low Validity — Face Validity	Content Validity — Objective Tests	Content Validity — Performance Tests	Test Item Validity (Objective Tests) — Distractor Analy.	Test Item Validity (Objective Tests) — Correl.	High Validity — Test Item Validity — Performance Tests Correlation	Predictive Validity
Organizational Needs	Return on Investment							X
	Improved Workforce							X
	Regulatory Requirements							X
	EEOC Requirements							X
Employee Traits	Promotion							X
	Performance Appraisal							X
	Improved Skills						X	
	Increased Knowledge				X	X		
	Self-improvement	X						
	Commercial Sale§	X	X	X	X	X	X	X

VALIDITY →   RELIABILITY*

§ All levels indicated because level is dependent on the commercial use for the course (see Chapter 5-5).
* When Predictive Validity is followed for an extended period of time.

2. Does the training result in increased or improved skills among employees to accomplish the organizational goals of the training?

> An improved workforce with higher levels of skills to get the job done better, faster, and more economically also requires you to be able to predict that the skills taught in the training directly result in speed and economy. Both speed and economy can be investigated separately, but increased speed at the sacrifice of improved performance is usually not a desirable outcome.

3. Does the training produce employees who are aware of government regulatory requirements?

> The main determination of the level of validity in training in regard to government regulations is whether the regulations require the employees to simply "be aware of" the regulations or are able to "perform" a skill or task better as a result of the training. The answer to this question will determine the level of validity that the training must achieve.

4. Does the training comply with the requirements of the EEOC Guidelines on fair employment practices and non-discrimination?

> There is a discussion and case examples of the EEOC and its relation to testing in Chapter 5-6. Basically, any prerequisite skills or knowledge, job requirements, or testing must be proven to be valid requirements that do not adversely impact any protected group. EEOC guidelines have been more broadly interpreted in the courts to include discrimination toward anyone by any type of testing or evaluation. The court cases cited demonstrate how courts typically rule in such cases.

If the measurement variables are designed to measure Employee Traits, you must still be able to prove that the traits accurately predict employee performance and that the training used to teach the knowledge and skills is valid. This is particularly important if the training is part of a career ladder required for an employee to advance in a company or if the training will be incorporated into a performance appraisal. If your company is a vendor for off-the-shelf training products, you should validate the training to the highest level or list in the documentation for the training at what levels the training has been validated and for which it can be used.

Some of the questions you will want to answer to determine validity are:

1. Does the training provide the skills necessary for employees to successfully complete the job into which they will be promoted?

Like organizational goals, the skills must accurately predict that the employee will be successful on the job in direct relation to successful completion of the training.

2. Does the training predict that employees will be able to perform their jobs better on the basis of successfully completing the training?

   Only if it is proven that the training is able to predict that successful completion will improve performance, can the skills be incorporated into a performance appraisal for the purposes of retaining employees or granting merit pay increases.

3. Does the training actually increase the knowledge and skills of the employees?

   The training must demonstrate that employees have increased knowledge based on the training, or that they have increased performance after the training, even if the increase will not be used for promotion, retention, or merit pay. This information lets the employer know that the training is minimally effective.

4. Does the training result in improved knowledge and skills based on the employees' own perceptions?

   Courses designed for self-improvement purposes require only that those who take the course believe that they have more knowledge and/or skills as a result of taking the training.

How To Evaluate

The objective of any good summative evaluation is to obtain accurate data that can be translated into meaningful information. Have your goals clearly in mind and then collect data that will achieve your goals. Don't overcollect information. Collecting all conceivable data in case you might need it will only confuse you when you go to interpret it. Overcollecting indicates that your goals are not clear enough.

You will need a good statistical package to analyze the raw data. We've used SPSS, produced by SPSS, Inc. in Chicago, Illinois. The Windows version is particularly easy to use and the documentation is excellent.

Many of the statistical tests that are used for norm-referenced statistical analysis do not work for Criterion Referenced Tests (CRT). A Norm Referenced Test (NRT) assumes a normal distribution among a randomly chosen segment of the general population. This type of distribution will show most people in the population to be clustered near the center of the group. There will be those who show skills to various degrees above and below that central point, in equal numbers. An example of an NRT is the Scholastic Aptitude Test (SAT) that is administered to high school students to predict their aptitude or probability of success for completing college.

However, if the training that you develop is to determine the level of proficiency attained by a group of students after receiving training on a specified set of skills, you are not looking for a normal distribution, you are looking for students who cluster around a central point that is much higher than that found among the general population. The increase in score on the test can be attributed to the fact that they were trained on the specific information in the course. The purpose of the testing is to separate those who have mastered the skills from those who have not. You would expect people to be clustered at a much higher level with smaller degrees above and below the clustered scores. Specific tests that are applicable to norm- or criterion-referenced analysis are listed in Chapter 5-3.

The mastery curve[14] has a high number of scores centered around the mastery level with small standard deviations and a negative or positive skew. When you plot the frequencies of scores on a Criterion-Referenced Test, you want a curve that looks like Figure 5-1-2 (negative) or one that has the tail of the curve to the right (positive).

Figure 5-1-3 shows the normal distribution you would expect if the general population performed the same task as the group shown in Figure 5-1-2. When you use a statistical test that is based on the normal distribution of scores to validate CRT, it is impossible to prove that differences exist because there is not enough variation between the scores of the persons who took the CRT.

---

[14] For those readers who are interested or want a good word to toss out at the next staff meeting, the mastery curve is known among statisticians as a "leptokurtic curve." We've defined it in the Glossary.

Figure 5-1-2
Range of Scores in CRT

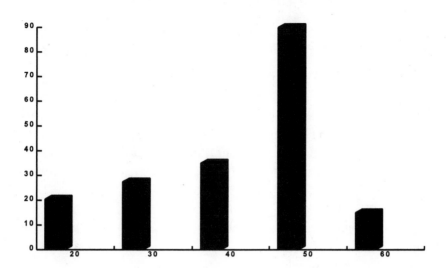

Mastery curve is determined by drawing a line connecting the top of each bar on the chart.

Figure 5-1-3
Range of Scores In NRT

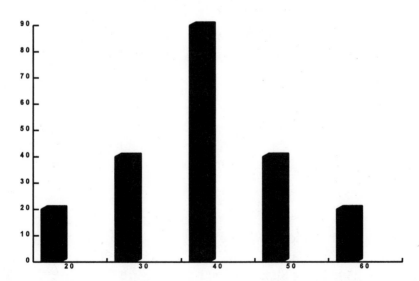

Normal Curve is determined by drawing a line connecting the top of each bar on the chart.

With this understanding of Norm-versus Criterion-Referenced Testing, let's look at two examples of the measurement variables compared to the purpose, and discuss how to achieve each level of validity required. This topic is covered in its entirety in Chapter 5-3, then related to testing outcomes in Chapter 5-5.

Measurement Variable	Purpose	Type of Test	Type of Validity
Employee Trait	Self-Improvement	Objective	Face Validity

Face Validity in the context of CBT course development means only that a course resembles any other course on the topic in its content. You can achieve this by having a SME review the course and simply state that the resemblance exists. If you didn't do this at the end of the Design Phase by showing the training plan to a SME, you can still do this now, but it might require some rework (which is difficult after the course is already programmed); so, we recommend you do this during the Design Phase.

You can measure the effectiveness of a course with what is commonly known as a "Smile Sheet" that contains questions that ask the students if they feel that they have the skills or knowledge that the training intended.

Moving to Increased Knowledge as a purpose for training brings quite a jump to the levels of validity required to prove that those who completed the course possess adequate levels of the required knowledge.

Measurement Variable	Purpose	Type of Test	Type of Validity
Employee Trait	Increased Knowledge	Objective	Content Validity Test Item Validity Difficulty Index

Content validity of the course material is established thorough the technical content review cycles conducted during formative evaluation, so test item content validity is what you need to establish here if it was not also done during the Design Phase. Here, again, programmed test questions are more difficult to change than on paper, so we recommend you establish test item validity during Design.

The methodology of establishing test item validity during Design is to use a panel of judges. Qualification to be a judge is based on subject matter knowledge expertise. A minimum of four judges should be used. Each judge is provided with a completed Test Specification Form (Figure 5-1-4) like the one found in the Application Tools section of this chapter for objective tests. The form must be completed with all pertinent information: the objective that the test question measures, the test question itself, and the criteria by which the question must be judged to meet the criteria.

Depending upon the level of criteria required, and the number of judges, you should do a frequency count on the number of judges who respond that the question meets the criteria. If you are using five judges, the criteria should be 80% (four of the five judges answer "Yes"). If you are using four judges, the criterion level should be 75% (three of the four judges answered "Yes"). If the level of knowledge required is extremely critical, you may choose 100% for the criteria regardless of how many judges you use.

Each question that achieves the criterion level is considered to have content validity. Those questions that do not reach criterion must be returned to the test writer for revision. Judges' comments are used to determine why an item was rejected. These rewritten questions must go through judging again. This process continues until all test questions reach the desired criterion level that establishes content validity.

If you are going to conduct distractor analysis and concurrent validity on the test items, then content validity can be achieved using statistical measures rather than the judging method. You don't need to do both.

RATIONALE

The decisions you make about the level of evaluation you conduct will determine the effectiveness of your training products. The effectiveness ultimately affects what you can guarantee your customers that the training will accomplish. The result of training must be to improve knowledge and, more importantly, performance. Evaluation of the types and to the extent we outlined above (and will expand upon in subsequent chapters) explains the optimum. We want you to know what the best training course can be and what its potential uses are after you have proven that it is effective.

If you develop only internal training for your company, you may think that you can escape with lower levels of evaluation. As a matter of fact, you may even hear this from your management.

You are mistaken, and management is mistaken. By making such a statement, you are both saying that you will settle for less effective training and lower performance for your company's employees.

Maybe some training is better than no training but no training is better than poor training. Unless you prove the effectiveness of your training with studies that follow up on those who complete the training, you can never claim that your efforts and the money that was expended by your customer was truly justified.

APPLICATION TOOLS

The Test Specification Form (Figure 5-1-4) can be used to determine test item content validity. This form and the example are designed for objective tests. They must be modified somewhat for performance tests where there are no distractors.

Figure 5-1-4
Test Specification Form
Objective Tests

> **Test item is valid: Yes __ No __**
> **(Check One)**

Terminal Objective: [Lesson Objective—Quiz; Enabling Objective—Embedded]

Test Item:

Item Attributes:

The stem of the sample item written to measure achievement in this objective should:

The responses for the sample item should:

Judge's Comments:

[EXAMPLE]
Test Specification Form
Objective Tests

> **Test item is valid: Yes __ No __**
> **(Check One)**

Terminal Objective:

Objective 1.3.3

Given a diagram of the electronic instrument, the student will discriminate each functional part by circling each major part with complete accuracy.

Test Item:

Circle the part of the diagram that shows the oscillator.

[PLACE DIAGRAM HERE]

Item Attributes:

The stem of the sample item written to measure achievement in this objective should:

1. State what the student is to do to demonstrate the knowledge.

2. State what part the student must circle to demonstrate the knowledge.

The responses for the sample item should:

Provide a diagram with the part that the student must circle readily visible and clearly able to be circled without interference or confusion with other parts.

Judge's Comments:

CHAPTER 5-2
COLLECTING INFORMATION

INTRODUCTION

Plan your evaluation thoroughly before you run it. Some things are recoverable because they are in the data and you only need to analyze them a different way, but some things might not be recoverable unless you run the evaluation again — costing time, money, and a delay in final implementation.

WHAT TO DO

Overcollecting Or Undercollecting Data

"Recoverability or forever lost" doesn't mean that you should run every test you can think of. What overcollecting will do, if you are not an experienced statistician, is give you so much information that you will be totally confused about what you end up with. We again emphasize that overcollecting data is an indicator that your objectives for the evaluation are not clear or that you need to better understand what you are doing.

If you have written your objectives using the process outlined in Chapter 2-10, you will have clear objectives. Review your objectives and determine what the final outcomes are. By using the information in this Unit, you should be able to accurately target what information you need and thus what data you need to collect.

How To Do It

Practice Session

Let's use two of the objectives from Chapter 2-10 on Writing Objectives and let you practice deciding what type of test to give in each situation. Try to determine the answers for yourself to each of the questions following the objective before you look at the Application Tools section of this chapter, where we give you the answers.

Practice Session 1

Objective:

> Given a diagram of the electronic instrument, the student will discriminate each functional part by circling each major part with complete accuracy.

Questions about this objective:
1. What must you evaluate?
2. How will you evaluate it?
3. What type of test will you use?
4. What level of validity do you need?
5. What data will you collect to prove that this objective is achieved and how will you collect it?
6. Why did you make these decisions?

Practice Session 2

Objective:

> Given an identified problem in the electrical system of an electronic instrument, the student will execute the diagnostic procedures by correctly attaching the volt meter to the ground and appropriate resistor or lead point with the correct ends on the correct terminals.

Questions about this objective:
1. What must you evaluate?
2. How will you evaluate it?
3. What type of test will you use?
4. What level of validity do you need?
5. What data will you collect to prove that this objective is achieved and how will you collect it?
6. Why did you make these decisions?

Constructing and Administering Questionnaires and Surveys

Questionnaires and surveys must be developed using principles of test development described in Chapter 5-4 regarding the degree of validity. These types of instruments must attain a minimum of content validity to return any degree of certainty about the information obtained.

Constructing Interview Instruments and Conducting Interviews

Again, as with questionnaires and surveys, a minimum of content validity must be attained for them to be useful.

Beyond that, there are certain conditions that are conducive to interviewing and interpersonal skills of interviewers that help draw interviewees out. Refer to Unit 2 for the procedures for conducting interviews.

Sample Size for Surveys, Questionnaires, and Interviews

"How many people should be surveyed?" is always among the top four questions that come up when the time arrives for conducting the surveys or for the interviews/mailing questionnaires. Refer to Unit 2 for information on sample size and how to calculate it.

Sampling some populations is difficult and there is always a tendency to cut corners. Some professionals and customers will point to some of the major rating organizations, such as the Harris Polling Organization, who sample a very small segment of the population and still achieve highly reliable results.

What many don't realize or stop to think is that professional rating corporations spend a great amount of money up front using very sophisticated computer systems to continually narrow and subdivide regions of the territory they plan to survey and the populations of those areas. They use and rely on systems that have been in place for many years and employ methodologies whose reliability has been constantly refined.

If your company has such sophisticated sampling equipment— if yours does, it is in a small minority — then you can use it to choose a sample size. If your company does not have the equipment and methodologies, then use the rule of 10% of the population.

Yes, it takes time; yes, it takes money. But do you and your customer want accurate information? If accuracy is not a concern, just guess and save the money!

Do it right or skip it. However, remember that you can have the best engineers in the world who can design and build the sturdiest, and even the most beautiful, bridges, but if they build them over the wrong river, they don't get anybody where they want to go.

Value of Surveys and Interviews

Don't totally discount the information that you can get from surveys and questionnaires. They yield very important information. The danger is when you totally rely on them to provide you with information. When you do use surveys and questionnaires, they need to be carefully constructed to give you the critical information you need. The sample forms in the Application Tools section of this chapter should give you an idea of the types of information you need to collect. Refer to Unit 2 on how to conduct interviews.

RATIONALE

Data must be collected systematically and thoroughly if it is going to produce information that is accurate and valuable. Cutting corners, overcollecting, under-collecting, or collecting incorrect information will produce results that don't provide answers to the questions you asked at the outset of the evaluation. Knowledge of research design, statistical measurement and interpretation is critical to arriving at the right conclusions.

Here is a "war story" that might give you some insight into how important collecting accurate data is. We once had a customer representative from a large corporation, for whom we developed a training course. We were required to prove the effectiveness of the training through two validation classes.

The customer representative had an advanced degree with background in testing and measurement. As part of the evaluation, he requested that we run a specific statistical correlation test that he could use to determine the effectiveness of the course. The problem was that the particular test he wanted was a test that began with the basic assumption that the test results would have a normal distribution. We had developed a Criterion-Referenced Test for the course to prove the mastery of the information in the course. You would not expect to find a normal distribution of scores on the tests for the course. As a matter of fact, if you did, the course would be *ineffective*.

By running the test that assumed a normal distribution, we would have run the risk of validating a course that was really not valid. A correlation test looks for a certain amount of agreement between the two variables you are measuring. In a criterion-referenced course, with small degrees of standard deviation, you would probably always find this condition to be true.

While we could have simply kept silent and run the test for the customer and possibly falsely proven that the course was effective, we chose to convince the customer — not an easy task when you are dealing with a representative who is an "expert" in testing and measurement — and ran a test that was more suited to criterion-referenced testing. He did not willingly admit that his test was not applicable to the situation, but succumbed when we raised it as a contractual issue that would have presented the dispute to a joint customer/client grievance committee.

Sometimes you have to risk losing a customer to protect the customer and your company. Pick your battles carefully. Don't go to war over a trivial issue.

This is a case where a gap existed in the knowledge of the customer representative that would have caused our company a lot of trouble (we ran the test the customer representative wanted just to see what would happen and it provided very low correlations). If we had not had the expertise in testing and measurement, we would have been completely steam-rolled by this "expert" and would have delivered an invalid course to the customer. This would have caused future problems for the customer's company as well as our own.

Of course, we could have always used the excuse that "we gave the customer what he wanted." However, when you are interested in repeat business, you had better have the knowledge to produce evaluations that are on target and will stand up to scrutiny of the most severe critic, even if it occasionally means having to take the time to educate the customer.

We learned something very important from this case. Before this, we had always thought "the customer was always right." We learned from this that "the customer is always the customer." Good customer relations are very important, but you can't give in to those customer demands that you *know* are in error.

APPLICATION TOOLS

The application Tools for this section include the answers to the Practice Sessions on determining how to evaluate objectives. The Survey Questionnaire and the Interview Form are examples of information-gathering instruments.

Answers to Practice Session 1

Objective:

Given a diagram of the electronic instrument, the student will discriminate each functional part by circling each major part with complete accuracy.

1. **What must you evaluate?**

    The student's ability to discriminate all of the major parts of an electronic instrument.

2. **How will you evaluate it?**

    Through the use of a diagram of the part that the student uses to circle each part.

3. **What type of test will you use?**

    A multiple choice type test that shows a picture of the entire electronic instrument, naming the part you want circled, and then checking to see if the correct part was circled.

4. **What level of validity do you need?**

    You need test item validity to the predictive level to determine not only that the test item can accurately measure the objective but that it can predict that the student can actually find the component on the actual instrument. (Component location will be done when the student must remove, replace, or otherwise repair that component on the instrument in a lab situation or on the job.) The test item that requires the student to circle the component is the first step to determining if the student has the knowledge; the final test is a performance test.

5. **What data will you collect to prove that this objective is achieved and how will you collect it?**

    Correcting the test and giving a score of + or − for this item on the objective test and by comparing the correct answer to this question by a student to his or her success on the lab exercise.

6. **Why did you make these decisions?**

    The reason for determining to use the objective, multiple choice test is because this is a knowledge-based question. It is more efficient to have students identify the parts on paper because you can have many students accomplish this objective at the same time. If you took each student into a lab situation or brought the electronic instrument into the classroom, you would have to observe each one of the students pointing to the part. This takes a lot of time. You will be able to determine if the knowledge is transferred when the students have to remove or replace, or otherwise repair, that part in a lab (covered by another objective written at the performance level).

The actual test item for this objective can be seen by looking at the completed Test Specifications in Chapter 5-1.

Answers to Practice Session 2

Objective:
>   Given an identified problem in the electrical system of an electronic instrument, the student will execute the diagnostic procedures by correctly attaching the volt meter to the ground and appropriate resistor or lead point with the correct ends on the correct terminals.

1. **What must you evaluate?**
>   The student's ability to actually use a volt meter.

2. **How will you evaluate it?**
>   Observe that the student can correctly attach the volt meter.

3. **What type of test will you use?**
>   Performance test where the student actually uses the volt meter.

4. **What level of validity do you need?**
>   Test Item Validity during performance testing that is conducted immediately following the training. In addition, predictive validity is required to confirm the task analysis that accomplishing this task is required for successful completion of the student's job after training. This is done by observing the student using the volt meter on the job when it is required and obtaining the correct diagnostic information coupled by the correct action based on the diagnostic information.

5. **What data will you collect to prove that this objective is achieved and how will you collect it?**
>   Use an observation checklist to determine that the student attached the volt meter correctly and give points to add to the overall score on the observation.

6. **Why did you make these decisions?**
>   The objective requires that the student actually use the volt meter by attaching it in the correct manner.

Figure 5-2-1
CBT Course Design Survey

Please complete this survey to give us feedback on your reactions and impressions of the CBT course you have just completed.

Name of Course _____

1.   Sex   (A) ___ M   (B) ___ F

2.   Age   (A) ___ 16-18   (B) ___ 19-25   (C) ___ 26-30
            (D) ___ 31-40   (E) ___ over 40

3.   Years with your company: _____

4.   Number of other CBT courses you have taken: _____

5.   Do you have problems identifying certain colors?   (A) ___ Yes   (B) ___ No

Key		
NA	–	not applicable
SA	–	strongly agree
A	–	agree
D	–	disagree
SD	–	strongly disagree

Indicate your response by circling your choice before each survey question using the key above. All responses are confidential. Your input will be used to evaluate the course.

CONTENT

NA SA A D SD   6. Directions were clear and easy to follow.

NA SA A D SD   7. The computer always provided help if I got confused.

NA SA A D SD   8. Objectives made it clear what I was supposed to learn.

NA SA A D SD   9. The content of the lessons followed the objectives.

NA SA A D SD   10. Quizzes were based on the content of the lesson.

NA SA A D SD   11. The material followed a logical sequence.

NA SA A D SD   12. Important terms were emphasized by highlighting or underlining.

NA SA A D SD   13. The vocabulary and length of sentences made the material easy to understand.

NA SA A D SD   14. Unfamiliar terms were defined.

NA SA A D SD   15. Enough examples of each concept were given.

NA SA A D SD   16. The examples were closely related to the material presented.

NA SA A D SD   17. Enough questions were asked throughout the presentation of the material for me to check my understanding of the lesson.

NA SA A D SD   18. If I missed a question, the program would re–teach or re–explain where I made my mistake.

NA SA A D SD   19. Questions were related to important skills rather than insignificant material.

NA SA A D SD   20. Material was summarized before a quiz.

NA SA A D SD   21. After a quiz, I could review questions I missed.

NA SA A D SD   22. I did not have to look at material I already knew.

NA SA A D SD   23. The menus were easy to use.

NA SA A D SD   24. Colors used on the screen were pleasant to look at.

Special Content Features

NA SA A D SD   25. It was easy to find information in the student manual.

NA SA A D SD   26. The student manual explained the information in a clear and simple manner.

NA SA A D SD   27. The student manual provided valuable information.

NA SA A D SD   28. The student manual was easy to read.

NA SA A D SD   29. The pictures and drawings in the student manual added valuable information.

GRAPHICS

NA SA A D SD   30. The charts and diagrams were easy to read.

NA SA A D SD   31. The charts and graphs were easy to understand.

NA SA A D SD   32. The text was easy to read.

NA SA A D SD   33. The pictures and drawings were clear.

VIDEO

NA SA A D SD   34. The colors on the screen were pleasant to look at.

NA SA A D SD   35. The background of each scene was appropriate and not distracting.

NA SA A D SD   36. The on–camera presenters were effective.

NA SA A D SD	37. The on–camera presenters were pleasant to watch but not distracting.
NA SA A D SD	38. The video image was clear.
NA SA A D SD	39. The video made the information clearer.

AUDIO

NA A B C D	40. The audio portions were easy to hear.
NA A B C D	41. The audio enhanced the text and the video.

Additional Comments

Write your answers in the space provided. Continue on the back, if necessary.

42.   What did you like best about the course?

43.   What did you like least about the course?

44.   What suggestions would you make to improve the course?

45.   Other comments.

Figure 5-2-2
Interview Form

A.   Overall

1. Did you enjoy taking the course by computer? Yes ___ No ___ Why or why not?

2. Do you think that you learned something significant from this CBT course? Yes ___ No ___. If Yes, What? If No, why not?

3. What other course(s) have you taken by computer? What did you think of them?

4. Would you take another CBT course? Yes ___ No ___ Why or why not?

5. What improvements would you recommend for this CBT course? Consider video, graphics, content, other.

B.   Motivation

1. Did any part(s) of the course catch and hold your interest making you want to continue? Yes ___ No ___ If Yes, which parts? If No, why not?

C.   Objectives

1. Did the beginning of each module clearly tell you what you were about to learn? Yes ___ No ___ If Yes, how was this done? If No, why not?

2. Did the lessons in the modules teach what they claimed to teach? Yes ___ No ___ Give one or two examples.

D.   Entry Behaviors

1. Did the Placement Test used before you started the course accurately test the things that you learned in the course? Yes ___ No ___ How?

2. Did the pretest for each module give you useful feedback about where your strengths and weaknesses were? Yes ___ No ___ How did it do this for you or what information did you need?

E.   Tests

1. Were test questions at the beginning and the end of the modules and lessons clear? Yes ___ No ___ Why or why not?

2. Were questions within the lessons clear? Yes ___ No ___ Why or why not?

3. Did you get useful feedback about why your answers were right or wrong?
Yes ___ No ___ How was this done?

F.   Instruction

1. Were the lessons presented in an interesting way? Yes ___ No ___ If Yes, how was this done? If No, why not?

2. Did the lessons give good information? Yes ___ No ___ How?

3. Did the questions in each lesson prepare you for the quizzes and the test?
Yes ___ No ___ How?

4. Were there enough opportunities to practice the skills you were to learn?
Yes ___ No ___ Why or Why not?

5. Were the video demonstrations clear and easy to understand? Yes ___ No ___ Give one or two examples.

CHAPTER 5-3
TEST VALIDITY

INTRODUCTION

Test item validity is determined through distractor analysis and statistical testing. Here's how you establish validity based on our own research (Lee, Roadman & Mamone, 1990).

WHAT TO DO

A Test Plan

You will need to develop a test plan. A test plan should grow out of Situational Analysis that determined how, where, and when the test will be administered. Artificially imposed restrictions placed on the test are not a good idea before assessment is completed. Artificially imposed restrictions are those found in Requests for Proposals (RFPs) or other unvalidated customer requirements. Examples are:

(1) predetermined test format (i.e., objective, multiple choice, etc.);
(2) predetermined number of questions;
(3) predetermined time for test administration; and
(4) predetermined ratio of class to test time.

You cannot determine test format before the end of analysis, and you cannot determine the number of test questions until after you have written your objectives. Time and ratios cannot be determined until after you decide on test format and number of questions. There must be a certain number of test questions for each objective in CRTs in order to give students an adequate opportunity to perform successfully. NRTs require only a sample of questions from the test item bank for each objective.

Of course, there will be certain limitations to the amount of time that can be spent on testing, but let Situational Analysis determine this. Even if the customer states certain conditions and you have to bid to those conditions, after contract award and your analysis, which may produce findings in opposition to the customer's up-front "guestimates," explain your reasoning to the customer for wanting to change the contract requirement. Once you see the number of objectives, you may decide the test format needs to be changed because there is a better method of evaluating the training. See the information on alternative bids in Unit 1.

Validity

You need to apply some type of qualitative or quantitative measure to the test to establish validity. You can use the quantitative data from the statistical tests described in the HOW TO DO IT section of this chapter to make qualitative judgments about the validity of your test.

How To Do It

Test Plan

Your objectives are written. Now you can develop a testing plan. The plan must include the following:

1. What type of test to administer.
2. How many questions are required.
3. How the test items will be weighed to determine how many from each objective to include on the test.
4. How to establish the validity of the test.

How Many Questions to Ask

Suppose that you have 50 terminal objectives for a course, and you determine that you should ask two questions per objective as a standard. This means that you would have a test with 100 questions. Remember, the students must have an adequate opportunity to demonstrate competence. Multiple questions per objective on a CRT increases this probability.

How Long the Test Will Take to Complete

How long will it take for students to complete this test? That will depend on the types of questions. Objective questions vary depending on the type (True/False, Matching, or Multiple Choice), how long the question stem will be, and how many distractors you will have. A good rule of thumb is to provide 30 seconds (one half minute) for each multiple choice question that has four distractors. Don't forget that you have to leave time in the test for students to read the directions or for you to explain them.

So, you have 50 objectives, two questions per objective, at 30 seconds per question plus about ten minutes to read and understand instructions. That means:

$$50 \times 2 \ @ \ .50 + 10 = 60 \text{ minute test}$$

Weighting Test Questions

But not all parts of a course carry equal weight. For instance, in a five hour course, if one section takes two hours to cover, it has more weight in the course than a section that takes one half hour. Here is a method to use to weight a test and then determine how many questions from each terminal objective go into the test.

If the two hour section of the course contains six of the terminal objectives, your job is simpler. At two questions per terminal objective, you simply put 12 questions from that section on the total test. But suppose you have one terminal objective for this two hour section? Well, you can count the number of Lesson Objectives and follow the same procedure just explained. Obviously the more

Lesson Objectives that must be taught, the longer the section, thus, the more weight in the course (see Table 5-3-1).

Table 5-3-1
Objective Weighting Matrix

Terminal Objective	Unit Where Covered	Time in Course	Comparative Amount of Content (%)	Weight	Number of Questions *	Test Time§
1	Unit 1	30 min	8.3	.08	1	.50
2	Unit 1	1.00 hr	16.7	.17	2	1.0
3	Unit 2	45 min	12.5	.13	2 (1.6)	1.0
4	Unit 3	15 min	4.2	.04	1 (.5)†	.5
5	Unit 4	2.00 hr	33.3	.33	4	2.0
6	Unit 5	1 hr 30 min	25.0	.25	3	1.5
Totals						
6	5	6 hr	100	100	13	6.5 min‡

* Assume two questions per objective if all weighed equally (6 Units x 2 Questions = 12 questions).
§ Assume multiple choice — .50 min per question.
† Must have a minimum of one question per objective.
‡ Does not include the time to read instructions.

Validity

Qualitative Measures

Frequency counts are a quantitative measure but require judgment to determine their benefit. Frequencies are easy to generate even if you don't use a statistical package just by counting the number of responses based on some standard (i.e., correct/incorrect). However, a statistical package generates the data much faster, especially for large numbers of cases.

For example, if you administer a performance test where students have multiple chances to successfully complete the task, you can perform a frequency count to determine how many attempts were required for most (whatever standard you want to use; i.e., 80 %) of the students to accomplish the task out of four tries. If the number is low, that task is valid. If there are some tasks that it takes 80% of the students four tries to accomplish, you had better check that item, as the task is probably not valid. Using the frequencies listed in the example below on calculating means, your results would be (see next page):

Item Number		Frequency		Percent	Point At Which Criteria Achieved	
1	=	4/11	or	36.4%		
2	=	7/11	or	64.0%		
3	=	8/11	or	73.0%		
4	=	10/11	or	91.0%	←	(80%)

This item needs to be carefully scrutinized. Criteria should be achieved in the first two attempts. You can calculate the mean (average) score of an item by totaling the responses and dividing the total by the number of responses.

Example:

Item Score	1	2	3	4	5
Responses	(4)	(3)	(1)	(2)	(1)

$$1 \times (4) = 4$$
$$2 \times (3) = 6$$
$$3 \times (1) = 3$$
$$4 \times (2) = 8$$
$$5 \times (1) = 5$$

Total = 26

Mean = 2.4

Quantitative Measures

There are other statistical measures that you can apply to determine validity. The trick is knowing which statistical tests to use, and how to interpret the data you receive. Here are some common statistical measures of validity with an explanation of when to use them and how to use them.

DISTRACTOR ANALYSIS

In Distractor Analysis, you need to determine whether there are questions that are being frequently missed by those who take the test and whether they are being drawn to one particular distractor (in the case of an objective test) that is causing them to get the question wrong. A statistical package can perform this task by simply analyzing the frequencies of certain answers that are given.

If the above condition exists for any question, professional judgment is then needed to determine where the problem exists that is causing students to answer a question this way. It may be a problem in the way the question is asked or it may be some inaccurate or confusing information in the course content.

But what about the questions that score with no correlation (0.00)? Well, then you must look at an index of the level of difficulty for that question. If all students got the question right or if all got it wrong, then the question is probably a poor question and needs to be rewritten. Compare questions with 0.00 correlation to your frequency tables.

How high should positive correlation be to be considered a valid question. A sufficient level of positive correlation for each question should be +.80, again based on the criticality of the knowledge — brain surgeon or management trainee. Low positive correlations will require distractor analysis and frequency counts.

Pretesting

When to use or not to use a pre-posttest? For either objective or performance tests, if students can test out of a course or particular units of a course based on pretest scores, that is a valid reason for using the pretest/posttest. If the training is highly technical and you are relatively assured, based on the analysis, that all students are beginning at the same level, there is no need for pretesting. If there were other forms of training provided to certain students in the past, or if their work experience provided some with higher levels of knowledge than others, a pre-posttest might be in order, but again only if students can test out of the training based on pretest scores.

The same criteria for pre-post-testing applies for performance as well as for objective tests. Pretest if the students can test out because analysis has determined that there are widely varying skills among the students. If there is no evidence of wide diversity in prerequisite skills, don't waste your time. It might be "nice to know" but it is not necessary.

Levels of Validity and How to Achieve Them

Table 5-3-2 lists the most common types of validity, explains how to achieve each, the importance, and where in the project phase you establish each type.

Table 5-3-2
Types of Validity

Types Of Validity	How to Accomplish	Importance	Phase
Face Validity	Formative evaluation where experts review the course materials and qualitatively validate that the course content approximates what a course on this subject should teach.	Minimum validity required to establish that a course teaches what it intends to teach or that a test measures what it claims to measure.	Design and/or Development
Content Validity	Formative evaluation where experts review the course materials and qualitatively validate that there is congruence between the objectives, content, and test items.	Minimum validity required if the course is used for certification of competence in a subject.	Design
Concurrent Validity	Quantitative summative evaluation measure of the similarities between two tests.	Establishes test item validity.	Evaluation
Construct Validity	Quantitative summative evaluation measure of a relationship between scores on a test and job performance.	Establishes positive relationship between test questions and the actual job performed.	Evaluation
Predictive Validity	Quantitative summative evaluation measure of the ability of a test to predict future success in a skill area.	Establishes validity of a test and ensures that a test positively correlates with the job performance it claims to measure (short term). Establishes reliability of a test or course (long term).	Evaluation
Interrater Agreement	Quantitative formative or summative evaluation measure of the ability of raters to agree on the successful performance of a task.	Establishes the confidence level that independent observations are consistent among raters.	Assessment/ Analysis or Evaluation

Validating performance tests requires the same procedures as for objective tests. However, there are usually no distractors to choose from. Rather, there is a checklist of the skills that must be performed, and an evaluator must check that the skill was performed correctly. In the example at the top of page 219, the employee trait requires all of the types of validity whether by objective test or by performance test. (Refer back to page 196 for the discussion of the measurement variables self-improvement and increased knowledge.)

Measurement Variable	Purpose	Type of Test	Type of Validity
Employee Trait	Increased Performance	Objective Performance	Content Validity Test Item Validity Difficulty Index Interrater Agreement

Content validity is best determined using judges. Point-biserial Correlation will tell you if the skills are consistently being performed by those who have mastered the task. Again, the difficulty index can be used for those performance items that produce low or no positive correlation.

Some Employee Traits and Organizational Needs must be validated at the highest level — predictive validity. What you must show in each of these cases is that the tests, whether knowledge or performance, can accurately predict that the person who completes the training will be successful on the job. What this really means is that you must be able to prove that those who fail the course would not be successful on the job.

This proof involves a very careful Assessment and Analysis of the tasks that the students who take the course will be trained on. Assessment has to establish that enough people who are already masters have been observed, interviewed, and rated, to establish the criteria for successful completion. You must use SMEs who are highly trained in interrater observation skills to perform the assessment and establish all levels of validation below predictive validity. Whether the tests are objective (based on knowledge acquired) or performance (based on ability to accomplish the skill), predictive validity must be established.

Once Analysis establishes the skills and the level of proficiency, you can use performance validation procedures to determine that all students are trained to the required proficiency level. You must then follow the students into the actual workplace and evaluate them at pre-established points over time, using the same evaluation instrument, to establish that adequate levels of proficiency are maintained. Predictive validity studies typically take place over an extended period of time. If your customer is really dedicated to improving employee performance and output, he or she will continue to collect data on the proficiency of his or her employees on the job. Chapter 5-6 explains why failure to demonstrate that employees need certain skills can cause problems for employers who use criteria to hire or exclude candidates for certain jobs.

Measurement Variable	Purpose	Type of Test	Type of Validity
Organizational Need	Return on Investment	Performance	Predictive

Justifying the ROI (see above chart) for a customer means proving that the cost of developing the training will reduce the overall cost of delivering training over time or that increasing proficiency will cut costs. Data the customer has collected up to the point where the new training is implemented will strengthen the case for justifying the training. Especially with CBT, the initial investment in hardware and having the training developed must be justified to boards of directors, or your company or team may not get any further contracts from that customer.

ROI relates only to the levels of validity in the respect that you must prove higher levels of proficiency once students complete the training and that proficiency is maintained over time (predictive validity). Once this is established, you can go on to demonstrate training effectiveness in dollars. Boards of directors understand the "bottom line" better than "performance increase" data. They will listen to the justification that the bottom line is positively impacted as a result of improved performance that can be linked to the training.

If the customer has not been collecting data on the costs of training but wants you to justify this aspect by the time the training is complete, your company must begin to collect the information you will need during Assessment/Analysis. Assessment and Analysis will tell you what information you have to collect and where to obtain the information.

To establish cost savings you will have to figure in all of the cost factors for the current training and compare that to the costs of developing and delivering the CBT; track the cost of delivering it over a period of time and then amortize the cost over a period of years to determine the break-even point, after which the savings begins.

Interrater Agreement

When observations are used to judge performance, interrater agreement must be added to train those who will conduct the rating. Interrater agreement means that all raters must all be able to view the same task and rate it nearly (with about 95% consistency or $p < .05$) the same.

Interrater agreement is established through practice having evaluators view the same performance task (either live or on video tape) and rate the tasks using the validated checklist. You can use a norm-referenced statistical test here to determine interrater agreement — a t-Test of statistical significance. If you establish an interrater correlation coefficient of +.90 or higher, you have a high degree of interrater agreement (+.95 is excellent — again, the criticality of what the raters are observing determines the degree of interrater agreement you need. Higher levels of agreement will take more training and longer to achieve). However, evaluators should be retrained on a regular basis if their evaluations will occur over an extended period of time because their judgments can be affected based on the number of students they observe over time.

Parallel Forms of Tests

You may have an instance where you need to develop parallel forms of tests. Parallel form test construction is determined through the similarity between the weight, content, and difficulty level of test items. Parallel forms of any test — objective or performance — must have the following characteristics:

(1) the same number of questions per objective;
(2) the same level of difficulty of each test item; and
(3) the same level of difficulty on the overall test.

Here's how to go about establishing parallel test validity.

(1) Provide a copy of the Directions for Developing Parallel Test Item Banks (Figure 5-3-1) to each judge.
(2) Provide a set of numbered test questions to the judges.
(3) List the weight of each terminal objective on the Parallel Test Item Bank Construction Form.
(4) Provide a set of numbered objectives with the Parallel Test Item Bank Construction Form (Figure 5-3-2) to a panel of SME judges who will determine the parallelism. Have the number of each terminal objective marked in the column for Terminal Objective before you give the form to the judges.
(5) Judges must match each terminal objective with two questions that they determine have an equal level of difficulty.

RATIONALE

Testing is typically what we do worst. The causes of poor testing stem from either lack of knowledge or lack of attention, or both. It's a circular construct: Testing results are the only justification for claiming that training is effective; → effective training solves the customer's problem; → solving problems creates satisfied customers → satisfied customers justify our existence; → our longevity allows us to produce more training programs that can be tested for their effectiveness. (See the illustration on the following page.)

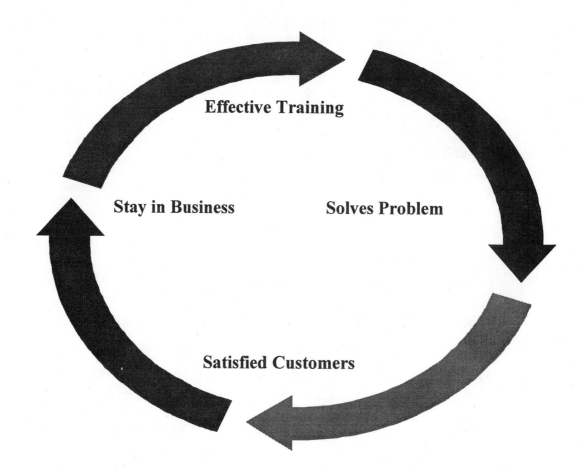

Effective Training

Stay in Business   Solves Problem

Satisfied Customers

Knowing what to test and how to do it to target the data that provides relevant information is a process that requires careful thought by persons with highly specialized skills. Your evaluation design may be very sound, but something as simple as choosing the wrong measure of what you are trying to prove may cause you to find significance where there is none or no significance where there actually is some. (In statistics the terms for finding significance where there is none or finding none where there is some is known as "Type 1" and "Type 2" Errors.)

APPLICATION TOOLS

The Application Tools for this chapter are those steps required to establish Parallel forms of tests and an example of a form you can use to complete the task.

Figure 5-3-1
Directions For Developing Parallel Test Item Banks

The purpose of this activity is to establish the content validity of two forms of the same test from the test item bank that you are provided.

Your task is to determine which test items are similar in their level of difficulty and the content of the questions.

Perform the following steps to complete your task:

1. A set of numbered objectives is supplied to you with the validation forms. The number of the terminal objective is already inserted in the column of the form marked Terminal Objective.

2. A set of numbered questions is also supplied to you. The weight of each objective is listed for you. The weight was previously determined using a formula that established the fractional part of the content of the entire course that each objective addresses. This would always total 1.0 (100%). This means that there must be as many test items on Test 1 as there are on Test 2 in proportion to the weight of the content of the course.

   Example: if one objective is listed as .5, then it should contain half of the questions for the test.

3. Read each test item and write the number of the item on the line beside the number of the terminal objective that it addresses and in the column marked Test Item.

4. You should find that there are an equal number of questions that address each Terminal Objective.

5. You should also find and agree that the level of difficulty is equal between the two items that are parallel.

6. When you are satisfied with your decisions, sign the bottom of the form and return it to (*name of person in charge of validation*).

Figure 5-3-2
Parallel Test Item Bank Construction Form

Project _____ Date _____

Evaluator _____

Terminal Objective Number	Weight	Test Item Number	Test Item Number	Test Item Number	Test Item Number	Same Level of Difficulty

I concur that the test items matched above are parallel in form.

_____
Signature

CHAPTER 5-4
USING APPROPRIATE MEASURES OF TRAINING'S EFFECTIVENESS

INTRODUCTION

You cannot use norm-referenced statistical measures to analyze CRT and vice versa. As we pointed out in the Rationale for Chapter 5-2 through our "war story," using the wrong measure will produce results that are erroneous.

All NRTs were at one time CRTs in their test item validation phase. The objective of norm-referencing is to establish a criterion with a mean of .50. This means that the average person for whom the test is designed will get the question correct, and that there are standard deviations of equal distance both above and below that mean or average.

Table 5-4-1 lists some statistical measurement tests and their appropriate use. Appendix D provides a more complete explanation of each test with information as to when each is appropriate with respect to the type of test you administer, the nature of the results you need, and the size of the group you will be testing (sample size).

ITEM ANALYSIS

Item analysis determines if the individual test items and the overall test are valid. Item analysis establishes the validity of test questions through the determination that those who performed best on the overall test also got a particular test item correct.

To perform an item analysis you must have two independent variables that can be compared in some way to make the determination about how good your test questions are. There are a number of statistical tests that will establish this for NRT and others for CRT.

Correlation

Correlations establish the relationship between two variables. The result is a number between –1.0 and +1.0. Numbers closer to +1.0 indicate a high positive correlation. Numbers closer to –1.0 indicate a high negative correlation. The higher the positive correlation, the better the test item. But what about questions that receive 0.00? You must then use the difficulty index to determine whether to include or exclude the item (see Chapter 5-3).

Here is an example of how correlation works and its value. A company we worked for developed an interactive video, basic mathematics course. As part of the course, there was a pretest and posttest to measure the increase in knowledge and skills obtained by the students as a result of taking the course. During the pretest, students could test out of certain modules by answering selected questions correctly on the diagnostic test, and were channeled into other modules if they incorrectly answered these selected questions. If the students failed the diagnostic pretest, they had yet another chance once they entered a module of instruction, through yet another mastery test. If students scored 90% on the mastery test, they could at this point skip the module, or choose to continue through it anyway.

But our company needed to know if the test measured the skills generally determined by experts to be required by students who have mastered basic mathematics skills. To determine this, the company had to answer the question "Does this test have a high degree of predictive validity?" The company began by administering the test they developed to groups of college freshmen (about 100) who had been determined by college placement tests to need remedial mathematics to succeed in their college courses. They also found that the mathematics test from a national high school equivalency exam had been well documented as having a high degree of validity and reliability. The company also administered this test to the same group of students.

By correlating the scores between the two tests — the course test with the standardized test — we determined that there was a high degree of correlation between the two tests. As a result, the company was able to make the claim that students who passed the posttest in the interactive video course had the mathematical knowledge and skills of students who have graduated from high school.

Distractor Analysis

Analyzing the answers that students give to a test is known as distractor analysis. In distractor analysis you must look for any questions that have received a low positive or negative correlation and determine if there is one particular distractor that drew the better students away from the correct answer. Find out which distractor is causing the problem and then qualitatively analyze why that distractor might be causing problems. Rewrite the distractor (and any others for that question that need clarity), re-administer the test, and perform the same correlation analyses. Frequency analysis will also provide this information.

If you are fortunate enough to have access to the students who answered the question incorrectly, ask them why they chose their particular answer. This is a very good source of feedback. However, when the students are not available, use the first method.

Rationale

If you want to cut a board to build a house, you have to measure the board accurately. Too long or too short, and the board is useless. To test the effectiveness of training you have to measure it accurately also. Although we have pointed out in Chapter 5-2 that student surveys have value, they are often used as

Table 5-4-1
Appropriate Statistical Measures

Test Name	Purpose	Application NRT	Application CRT	Type Corr.	Type Sig.	Sample Requirements
Biserial	1 continuous/ 1 dichotomy	√	√	√		RSS[15]
Chi-square	1 continuous/ 1 dichotomy		√		√	RSS
Kendall's tau	2 continuous variables	√		√		$n < 10$
Kuder Richardson (KR-20)	measure of equal difficulty	√	√	√		RSS
Mann Whitney	compare unequal groups	√	√		√	RSS
Pearson Product Moment (Pearson r)	2 continuous variables	√		√		RSS
Phi Coefficient Φ	2 true dichotomies			√		RSS
Point-biserial	1 continuous/ 1 true dichotomy		√	√		RSS
Rank Difference	2 continuous variables	√		√		$n < 30$
Analysis of Variance (ANOVA)	significance between more than 2 means	√	√		√	RSS
t-Test	significance between 2 means	√			√	RSS

the sole source of feedback. These "Smile Sheets" are not solid evidence of course effectiveness. They may, to some degree, be evidence of students' pleasure with the course, their impressions of the instructor and the instruction; however, there are many factors that affect their responses (i.e., they don't want to say anything to hurt the instructor because (s)he's a nice person; they don't find it any better or worse than most courses they have taken).

Solid judgment by experts who can judge effective training, backed by quantitative measures of that effectiveness, will ultimately determine what "good" instruction is. Increased use of hard data will also make course developers more accountable for what they write and deliver. Let's all welcome that rather than become too

---

[15] Representative Sample Size. As we explain in the discussion of sample size, a representative sample is approximately 10% of the population unless you have very sophisticated sample selection procedures available for your use.

"messianic" and feel that because we wrote it, it must be good because we are, after all, "experts" in the field. Let the hard data prove that we are experts.

APPLICATION TOOLS

Appendix D contains a complete explanation of each of the tests described in Table 5-4-1.

CHAPTER 5-5
TESTING OUTCOMES

INTRODUCTION

This chapter uses Figure 5-1-1 from Chapter 5-1 to explore which type of test is best suited for the training with respect to how accurately it measures the purpose of the training. We will also discuss the drawbacks of using tests other than those recommended. You must make the decisions outlined in this chapter before you can choose the test you need to use.

HOW TO CHOOSE THE RIGHT TEST

Here are the guidelines and rationale you can use to make decisions regarding the type of test to use based on your purpose and the level of validity required.

Purpose	Level of Validity Required	Type of Test
Return on Investment (ROI)	Predictive Validity (Test-Retest Reliability)	Performance Test

A performance test is the very best measure of the return on investment of training. However, to determine the ROI, this performance test cannot be a single, one shot, independent measure at the end of a course. Students who complete the course must be followed into the field and observed on a regular basis over time to observe if they are using the skills taught during the training. If you can determine that they are using the skills, then determine what cost savings can be directly attributed to the use of the skills.

There are a number of things to consider when determining cost savings:

(1) original cost of development of the training;
(2) cost of delivering the training;
(3) cost of having the employee off the job during training (direct costs, salary, indirect costs, amount of revenue the employee would be generating if on the job);
(4) cost of having observers trained and sent into the field to observe that the skills are being used;
(5) revenues saved/generated as a result of the use of the training; and
(6) cost of writing the report on the follow-up.

Purpose	Level of Validity Required	Type of Test
Improved Workforce	Predictive Validity (Test-Retest Reliability)	Performance Test

Evaluating an improved workforce is very much like return on investment, but here the effectiveness of the workforce, rather cost elements, is evaluated. Again, long-term follow-up is required at regular intervals to determine if the skills are being used correctly.

There are a number of things to consider when determining the improvement of the workforce:

1. Is less time being spent on the activity during the performance of the job?
2. Is the level of proficiency significantly improved even though the time has decreased?

Purpose	Level of Validity Required	Type of Test
Regulatory Requirements	Predictive Validity	Performance Test
		Simulation
		Objective Test

Depending upon the type of regulation, any of the three types of tests may be applied. If the regulation involves something that the employee must be able to perform, then a performance test is required. If the regulation requires that an employee know certain information, then a low-level simulations using scenarios, audio, video, graphics, with objective test questions can be used. If the regulation requires only that information be provided to the employees, but you must certify that they have taken the course and are "aware of" the information for their own protection or benefit as well as the company's, then an objective test will suffice. Remember, however, that you must establish the correct level of validity and reliability on the applied tests to determine that it predicts that the employee knows or can perform the regulation.

Purpose	Level of Validity Required	Type of Test
EEOC Requirements	Predictive Validity	Simulation
	Performance Test	Objective Test

If the purpose of the test is to determine that employees have the ability to use and carry out EEOC regulations, then performance tests or low-level simulations are recommended that require students to demonstrate their use or implementation of the particular regulatory requirements. If the purpose of the test is to determine that employees have certain knowledge (i.e., their rights regarding employment fair practices) then an objective test is sufficient. This objective test may take any form as long as it achieves the required level of validity through continuous record keeping of the scores of those who take the test.

Purpose	Level of Validity Required	Type of Test
Promotion	Predictive Validity	Objective Test

Tests administered for the purpose of promotion must demonstrate that they can accurately predict success in the new position. Performance tests would be preferable, but it is sometimes difficult to put an individual in a position and then determine if he or she can carry out the responsibilities of the job. There are some standardized performance tests that claim to predict management abilities. Consult Buros' *Mental Measurements Yearbook* (1993) for examples of these tests and their levels of validity and reliability.

A much more practical way is to administer an objective test that has been thoroughly validated that can predict success (also see Buros). If you develop the test yourself, validate it by administering it to a large number of individuals who are in that position. Then the success of those who are promoted through the use of the test must be tracked over a long period of time. The test must be revalidated as requirements for the position change. This revalidation requires constant scrutiny on a regular basis. As companies reorganize and positions are consolidated, job descriptions change and more responsibilities and duties are vested in one individual. Organizational flattening requires changes to the test.

Purpose	Level of Validity Required	Type of Test
Performance Appraisal	Predictive Validity	Performance Test

The best measures of a job holder's ability to perform the required duties is a performance appraisal form that is well validated to ensure that it lists essential elements for performing the duties of the job. Validation occurs in much the same manner as objective tests for promotion but at the performance level. Static performance rating sheets that are purchased or developed internally, but not validated, are of little use when challenged in court.

Purpose	Level of Validity Required	Type of Test
Improved Skills	Test Item Validity	Performance Test

Where skills are expected to be improved because of the training but there is no element of promotion or performance appraisal, performance tests can be developed and validated through pilot studies used on a large number of the target population that has been trained. Validation through test item analysis establishes only the internal consistency of the individual items on the test when performed by each of the subjects who take the test. This is done through correlational statistical analysis (covered in Chapter 5-4).

Purpose	Level of Validity Required	Type of Test
Increased Knowledge	Test Item Validity	Objective Test

Where proving increased knowledge is the requirement, distractor analysis and Point-biserial correlation (for CRT) will establish the internal consistency of the test much as for a test of improved skills. Tests for increased knowledge are validated the same way as those for improved skills — through administering it to large numbers in the population and tracking the consistency of the findings which ultimately results in the test becoming an NRT.

Purpose	Level of Validity Required	Type of Test
Self-improvement	Face Validity	Any Type

Self-improvement courses taken for your own particular purpose need only be consistent with other courses on the same topic. A SME need only look at the course and certify that it looks like other courses on this topic. This can be anything from a chess simulator, to a video game, to a self-instructional course on any number of special interest topics.

Purpose	Level of Validity Required	Type of Test
Commercial Sale	Predictive Validity	Any type depending upon the course content and purpose.

When you work for a commercial training company that develops off-the-shelf training products, you don't know what the purchaser intends to use the training for. No matter what type of test you develop — simulations or objective — the highest level of confidence is predictive validity that measures the material against the purpose it was designed for. Lower levels than predictive validity can be established as long as the course documentation clearly identifies this for the purchaser. Potential buyers should be made aware of what the test can and cannot be used for.

RATIONALE

The guiding factor regarding the type of test to use is what you want the students to "possess" in knowledge, skills, or attitudes after they complete the training. Knowing what to evaluate, how to evaluate it, and the correct test to use starts to make sense when you add the dimension of the "purpose" of the test. You have to know what it is you intend to prove by testing and the purpose of the course.

APPLICATION TOOLS

Table 5-5-1 is a summary of all of the validity charts in this chapter. Note that these further explain the matrix (Figure 5-1-1) in Chapter 5-1.

Table 5-5-1
Summary Validity Table

Organizational Need		
Purpose Return on Investment (ROI)	**Level of Validity Required** Predictive Validity (Test-Retest Reliability)	**Type of Test** Performance Test
Purpose Improved Workforce	**Level of Validity Required** Predictive Validity (Test-Retest Reliability)	**Type of Test** Performance Test
Purpose Regulatory Requirements	**Level of Validity Required** Predictive Validity	**Type of Test** Performance Test Simulation Objective Test
Purpose EEOC Requirements	**Level of Validity Required** Predictive Validity	**Type of Test** Simulation Performance Test Objective Test

(Continued on next page)

Table 5-5-1
(Continued)

Employee Trait		
Purpose Promotion	**Level of Validity Required** Predictive Validity	**Type of Test** Objective Test
Purpose Performance Appraisal	**Level of Validity Required** Predictive Validity	**Type of Test** Performance Test
Purpose Improved Skills	**Level of Validity Required** Test Item Validity	**Type of Test** Performance Test
Purpose Increased Knowledge	**Level of Validity Required** Test Item Validity	**Type of Test** Objective Test
Purpose Self-improvement	**Level of Validity Required** Face Validity	**Type of Test** Any Type
Purpose Commercial Sale	**Level of Validity Required** Predictive Validity	**Type of Test** Any type depending upon the course content and purpose.

CHAPTER 5-6
LEGAL AND ETHICAL ISSUES

INTRODUCTION

However you decide to test, be sure that the testing criteria match (are congruent with) the desired performance and the content and methodology of the course. There must be congruence between the objective, the way the course is taught, and the way the testing is to proceed.

EEOC GUIDELINES

Legal difficulties can arise from inadequate test validation. Procedures are outlined here and are based upon both government guidelines and court precedence. The *Uniform Guidelines on Employee Selection Procedures*, commonly known as "The Guidelines," adopted by the Equal Employment Opportunity Commission (EEOC) in 1978 and subsequently adopted by all Federal agencies, have become the de facto standard for evaluating the testing decision that led to the end of discriminatory hiring patterns. However, mounting case law based on the EEOC Guidelines has broadened the intended use to include fair testing practices.

The Guidelines specifically address three types of validity:

(1) criterion-related,
(2) content,
(3) construct.

Section 15 of the Guidelines addresses the issues of:

(1) how the job was analyzed or reviewed and what information was obtained from this job analysis or review;
(2) criterion-related validity as a description of the criterion measures of job performance; how and why they were selected; how they were used to evaluate employees; a description of the statistical methods used to determine whether scores on the selection procedures are related to scores on the criterion measures of job performance, and the results of statistical calculations; and
(3) content validity as a description of the content of the job, as identified from the job analysis; a description of the procedure by which content was selected for inclusion on the test, and **evidence demonstrating that the tested content resulting from the selection procedure is a representative sample of the content of the job** (emphasis added).

The Guidelines conclude that:

> "...[a company] continuing to use a test that has question-
> able validity increases the risk that [a company] will be
> found to be engaged in discriminatory practices and will be
> liable for back pay, awards, plaintiff's attorney's fees, loss
> of Federal contracts, subcontracts or grants, and the like."

Although the Guidelines refer to validation of tests for the purpose of evaluating students, tests with questionable validity cannot be used to judge the effectiveness of a course since it is the *students* who have to be tested to achieve testing results.

LITIGATION AND CONSENT DECREES

Litigated cases are those that are argued before a judge, and sometimes a jury, in open court. Consent Decrees are mutual agreements between two parties that have the effect of law but are settled without argument before a judge and jury. The decisions handed down by the courts through litigation or as a result of these decrees become a matter of public record and can be used in subsequent cases.

The tough ones are the many cases settled out of court, which outnumber consent decrees or litigation. These never become public record and cannot be used as legal precedent. As a result, there are many issues where companies have decided they are at fault, but, rather than ever having their feet held to the fire sometime in the future because they lost in court or consented to a settlement, will settle with an individual with the stipulations that neither side disclose the issues, the agreement, or the amount of the settlement. In this way the company accepts no "guilt" in the matter.

Case law has established precedence that supports the Guidelines with respect to validation of tests and testing procedures that must match the performance required on the job.

Court Cases

The following cases are examples of litigation and consent decrees:

Guardians Assn., New York City Police Department v. Civil Service Commission, City of New York (CA 2 (1980) rem 19:121; 23:677) 23 FEP Cases 677 ruled that the city had not established that the entry-level examination that discriminated against Black and Hispanic applicants had content or criterion validity. Further, the validation technique for purposes of determining compliance of the test can best be selected by a functional approach that focuses on the nature of the job. Content validity [alone] remains inappropriate for tests that measure knowledge of factual information if that measure of knowledge of factual information will be fully acquired in the training program.

Vulcan Pioneers Inc. v. New Jersey Department of Civil Service (CA 3, 11-10-87) 53 FEP Cases 703 where the U.S. Court of Appeals upheld a lower court ruling against Vulcan that the [lower] court properly found that job analysis did not meet professional standards, that there were flaws in the contents of the tests, and that tests were not appropriate for ranking candidates.

Bernard v. Gulf Oil Corp. (CA 5, 3-22-88) 49 FEP Cases 1855 where the U.S. Court of Appeals stated that biased tests are impermissible unless shown to be predictive of or correlated with elements of work behavior that comprise or are relevant to the job or jobs for which candidates are being evaluated.

Pandazides v. Virginia Board of Education (CA 4, 10-10-89) 56 FEP Cases 1587 where the U.S. Court of Appeals reversed a decision of a lower court disallowing exclusion of a teacher to obtain a teaching certificate when the court made no determination as to whether the National Teachers Examination represented essential functions of the job.

Evans v. City of Evanston (DC NI11, 8-19-88) 47 FEP Cases 1723 where the U.S. District Court upheld the city's use of a test of physical agility as part of the requirement for hiring firefighters because it had documented the need for performance in the job analysis and because the test had been administered to many incumbent firefighters.

Police Officers for Equal Rights v. the City of Columbus, Ohio (CA 6, 10-22-90) 54 FEP Cases 276 where the U.S. Court of Appeals upheld the use of a knowledge-based test when expert testimony was produced that the test was valid due to the positive correlation between the skills tested and job performance because there was a sufficient spread among candidates' scores.

Houston Chapter of the International Association of Black Professional Firefighters v City of Houston, Texas, (DC STexas, 5-6-91) 56 FEP Cases 445 where the U.S. District Court's consent decree declared that the elimination of questions that are biased to certain minorities does not unnecessarily trammel the interest of non-minority firefighters, where the elimination of the questions will more closely relate the test to job performance.

ETHICAL ISSUES

Beyond the legal obligations to your customer and your students, you have a moral business obligation to provide training that teaches what the students need to know, to the level that they need to know it. Once students complete your training they should be confident that they know or can do what they were taught. If they can't, they fail, but you also fail. However, their failure might mean the difference between promotion and no promotion; a raise or no raise; a job or unemployment. What if the failure comes from faulty training or testing, not their own lack of skills? Evaluation establishes the soundness of the training and provides you with the level of confidence you need to be reassured that you are providing the best training possible.

Unit 5 References

These are specific references for the chapters in this unit. For additional resources on topics in this unit, see the Bibliography.

Chapter 5-1

Hagan, E. & Thorndike, R. (1969). *Measurement and Evaluation in Education.* Third Edition. New York: John Wiley & Sons.

Lee, W. (1990). Evaluating Interactive Video Training Ensures Instructional Soundness. *Performance & Instruction*, 29(5), pp. 17-20.

Lee, W. (1990). *Training Evaluation Hierarchy.* Washington, DC: Library of Congress. Copyright No. TXu 401-552.

Lee, W. (1991). *The Instructional Design Process.* Washington, DC: Library of Congress. Copyright No. TXu 495-988.

Lee, W. (1994) Ensuring Instructional Effectiveness Through Sound Evaluation Strategies. *Proceedings of the 1994 International SALT Conference.* Orlando, FL.

Shrock, S. & Coscarelli, W. (1989). *Criterion-Referenced Test Development: Technical and Legal Guidelines for Corporate Training.* Reading, MA: Addison-Wesley Publishing Co.

Chapter 5-2

Borg, W. & Gall, M. (1983). *Educational Research: An Introduction.* Fourth Edition. New York: Longman.

Chapter 5-3

Borg, W. & Gall, M. (1983). *Educational Research: An Introduction.* Fourth Edition. New York: Longman.

Lee, W., Roadman, K., & Mamone, R. (1990). *Training Evaluation Model.* Washington, DC: Library of Congress. Copyright No. TXu 455-182.

Martuza, V. (1977). *Applying Norm-Referenced and Criterion-Referenced Measurement in Education.* Boston, MA: Allyn & Bacon.

Shrock, S. & Coscarelli, W. (1989). *Criterion-Referenced Test Development: Technical and Legal Guidelines for Corporate Training.* Reading, MA: Addison-Wesley Publishing Co.

Chapter 5-4

Borg, W. & Gall, M. (1983). *Educational Research: An Introduction*. Fourth Edition. New York: Longman.

Lee, W. & Roadman, K. (1991). Linking Needs Assessment to Performance Based Evaluation. *Performance & Instruction*, 30(6), pp. 4-6.

Martuza, V. (1977). *Applying Norm-Referenced and Criterion-Referenced Measurement in Education*. Boston, MA: Allyn & Bacon.

Chapter 5-5

Buros, O. (1993). *Mental Measurements Yearbook*. Highland Park, NJ: Gryphon Press.

Chapter 5-6

Equal Employment Opportunity Commission, U.S. Civil Service Commission. U. S. Department of Labor & U.S. Department of Justice. (1978). Uniform Guidelines on Employee Selection Procedures. Washington, D.C.: *Federal Register*.

Shrock, S. & Coscarelli, W. (1989). *Criterion-Referenced Test Development: Technical and Legal Guidelines for Corporate Training*. Reading, MA: Addison-Wesley Publishing Co.

BIBLIOGRAPHY

In addition to the sources noted in the chapters of this book, the following works will be helpful to persons and teams engaged in CBT.

Bailey, G., Editor. (1993). *Computer-Based Integrated Learning Systems*. Englewood Cliffs, NJ: Educational Technology Publications.

Behrman, M., Editor. (1988). *Integrating Computers into the Curriculum: A Handbook for Special Educators*. Boston: Little, Brown & Co.

Briggs, L., Gustafson, K., & Tillman, M., Editors. (1991). *Instructional Design: Principles and Applications*. Second Edition. Englewood Cliffs, NJ: Educational Technology Publications.

Briggs, L. & Wager, W. (1981). *Handbook of Procedures for the Design of Instruction*. Second Edition. Englewood Cliffs, NJ: Educational Technology Publications.

Butler, F. (1972). *Instructional Systems Development for Vocational and Technical Training*. Englewood Cliffs, NJ: Educational Technology Publications.

Carlisle, K. (1986). *Analyzing Jobs and Tasks*. Englewood Cliffs, NJ: Educational Technology Publications.

Dempsey, J. & Sales, G., Editors. (1993). *Interactive Instruction and Feedback*. Englewood Cliffs, NJ: Educational Technology Publications.

Fleming, M. & Levie, W. H., Editors. (1993). *Instructional Message Design: Principles from the Behavioral and Cognitive Sciences*. Englewood Cliffs, NJ: Educational Technology Publications.

Gagné, R. (1985). *The Conditions of Learning and Theory of Instruction*. Fourth Edition. New York: Holt, Rinehart, & Winston.

Gay, R. (1981). *Educational Research*. Columbus, OH: Charles E. Merrill Publishing Co.

Gayeski, D., Editor. (1993). *Multimedia for Learning: Development, Application, Evaluation*. Englewood Cliffs, NJ: Educational Technology Publications.

Haladyna, T. M. (1994). *Developing and Validating Multiple-Choice Test Items*. Hillsdale, NJ: Lawrence Erlbaum.

Hannum, W. & Hansen, C. (1989). *Instructional Systems Development in Large Organizations*. Englewood Cliffs, NJ: Educational Technology Publications.

Horton, W. (1990). *Designing and Writing Online Documentation: Help Files to Hypertext.* New York: John Wiley & Sons.

Imke, S. (1991). *Interactive Video Management and Production.* Englewood Cliffs, NJ: Educational Technology Publications.

Jones, M. (1989). *Human-Computer Interaction: A Design Guide.* Englewood Cliffs, NJ: Educational Technology Publications.

Kaufman, R., Rojas, A., & Mayer, H. (1993). *Needs Assessment: A User's Guide.* Englewood Cliffs, NJ: Educational Technology Publications.

Lee, W. (1990). Bridging the Gap With IVD. *Training & Development Journal,* 44(3), pp. 63–65.

Lee, W. (1990). Evaluating Interactive Video Training Ensures Instructional Soundness. *Performance & Instruction,* 29(5), pp. 17–20.

Lee, W. (1990). Maximizing Human Performance Through Simulation Training. *Performance & Instruction,* 29(9), pp. 20–21.

Lee, W. (1993). The Missing Phase in the ISD Model. *Performance & Instruction,* 32(10), pp. 5–7.

Lee, W. (1993). The Parable of Concurrent Development. *Performance & Instruction,* 32(8), pp. 12–13.

Leshin, C., Pollock, J., & Reigeluth, C. (1992). *Instructional Design Strategies and Tactics.* Englewood Cliffs, NJ: Educational Technology Publications.

Lorber, M. & Pierce, W. (1983). *Objectives, Methods, and Evaluation for Secondary Teaching.* Second Edition. Englewood Cliffs, NJ: Prentice-Hall.

Martin, B. & Briggs, L. (1986). *Affective and Cognitive Domains: Integration for Instruction and Research.* Englewood Cliffs, NJ: Educational Technology Publications.

McFarland, T. & Parker, O. (1990). *Expert Systems in Education and Training.* Englewood Cliffs, NJ: Educational Technology Publications.

Merrill, M. D. (1994). *Instructional Design Theory.* D. Twitchell, Editor. Englewood Cliffs, NJ: Educational Technology Publications.

Pettersson, R. (1993). *Visual Information.* Second Edition. Englewood Cliffs, NJ: Educational Technology Publications.

Phillips, J. (1991). *Handbook of Training Evaluation and Measurement Methods*. Second Edition. Houston, TX: Gulf Publishing Company.

Priestley, M. (1982). *Performance Assessment in Education and Training: Alternative Techniques*. Englewood Cliffs, NJ: Educational Technology Publications.

Rossett, A. (1987). *Training Needs Assessment.* Englewood Cliffs, NJ: Educational Technology Publications.

Schwier, R. (1987). *Interactive Video.* Englewood Cliffs, NJ: Educational Technology Publications.

Schwier, R. & Misanchuk, E. (1993). *Interactive Multimedia Instruction.* Englewood Cliffs, NJ: Educational Technology Publications.

Shneiderman, B. (1987). *Designing the User Interface: Strategies for Effective Human-Computer Interaction.* Reading, MA: Addison-Wesley Publishing Company.

Spector, J., Polson, M., & Muraida, D., Editors. (1993). *Automating Instructional Design: Concepts and Issues.* Englewood Cliffs, NJ: Educational Technology Publications.

Stevens, G. & Stevens, E. (1995). *Designing Electronic Performance Support Tools: Improving Workplace Performance with Hypertext, Hypermedia, and Multimedia.* Englewood Cliffs, NJ: Educational Technology Publications.

Towne, D. M. (1995). *Learning and Instruction in Simulation Environments.* Englewood Cliffs, NJ: Educational Technology Publications.

Wileman, R. (1993). *Visual Communicating.* Englewood Cliffs, NJ: Educational Technology Publications.

Wolfe, P. *et al.* (1991). *Job Task Analysis: Guide to Good Practice.* Englewood Cliffs, NJ: Educational Technology Publications.

APPENDIX A

TERMINAL OBJECTIVE VERB LIST
(Suitable for CBT)

Terminal Objective Verb List[*]

Skill	Verb	Definition
Discrimination	alter	to change
	arrange	to mentally order or classify in categories
	circle	to indicate understanding by encircling
	describe	to characterize qualities
	discover	to detect the true character
	divide	to separate into two or more parts or groups
	isolate	to set apart
	point	to make known or visible
	segregate	to separate or set apart from
	separate	to set apart
	set apart	to reserve to a particular use
	show	to point out a difference
	sort	to mentally group on the basis of common characteristics
	split	to mentally divide into parts or portions
	write/type	to put in print
Concrete Concept	arrange	to place in an orderly manner; to classify into categories
	call	to make a request
	catalog	to classify material
	combine	to synthesize in order to form a whole
	connect	to make a mental connection
	describe	to represent or give an account
	duplicate	to produce something equal to
	gather	to bring together or collect
	group	to form a complete unit from two or more parts; to classify; to mentally join or fasten together
	index	to list items in order to lead to a fact or conclusion
	inspect	to observe or take note of
	itemize	to detail or particularize

[*] Order matches the hierarchical levels of Gagné's learned capabilities as noted in Chapter 2-10.

Skill	Verb	Definition
Concrete Concept (Continued)	join	to put together to form a unit
	label	to describe or designate
	link	to mentally connect
	list	to inventory traits, preferences, attitudes, interests, or abilities that evaluate characteristics or skills
	mark	to distinguish a trait or quality
	match	to equate
	name	to label; to mention explicitly
	narrate	to relate in detail
	place	to distribute in an orderly manner
	point	to indicate; to assign
	repeat	to summarize principle points
	select	to choose by preference from a number or group
	sort	to arrange in groups according to predetermined specifications
	state	to verbalize
	tell	to relate or give an account of
	unite	to coordinate or blend
Defined Concept	alphabetize	to arrange alphabetically
	arrange	to put in order
	change	to modify or make fit
	evaluate	to appraise the worth of
	file	to arrange in order according to specified characteristics
	group	to combine according to certain specifications
	index	to classify according to certain characteristics
	list	to place in a specified category
	measure	to make determinations based on standard criteria
	order	to systematize
	organize	to form into a coherent unit
	pigeonhole	to assign to a category or classify
	rank	to orderly arrange
	rate	to assign a value; to estimate

Skill	Verb	Definition
Defined Concept (Continued)	record	to make a record of
	score	to assign a value to
	sort	to distribute into groups according to specified characteristics
	survey	to examine a condition or appraise
	weigh	to consider carefully or evaluate
	write/type	to put in print
Rule	announce	to make known or proclaim
	categorize	to separate according to specified characteristics
	coach	to instruct beforehand
	corroborate	to support with evidence
	define	to fix or mark limits
	depict	to decipher or make meaning from
	describe	to represent or give an account
	disclose	to uncover or make known; to reveal
	display	to exhibit or make evident
	divulge	to make public, unveil, or reveal
	explain	to tell, educate, or train
	expose	to portray, reveal, or draw forth
	extricate	to untangle or straighten; to pull from
	locate	to find; to place in a location or category
	organize	to arrange or form into a coherent unit; to integrate
	paint	to make a representation or give an example
	place	to situate or locate
	present	to show
	proclaim	to give an outward indication of
	prove	to authenticate
	relate	to tell
	reveal	to divulge or make known
	separate	to break up or resolve
	show	to demonstrate clearly or make clear
	state	to declare or affirm
	summarize	to state concisely

Skill	Verb	Definition
Rule (Continued)	teach	to instruct or train
	tell	to give an account of
	tutor	to coach or guide, usually in a particular subject
	unfold	to open to view; to reveal
	verify	to establish truth, accuracy, or reality; to confirm
Problem Solving	acquire	to come to have possession of
	arrive	to appear; to reach a predetermined or undetermined point
	assemble	to fit together
	build	to construct or form
	collect	to bring together into one body or place
	complete	to finish
	compose	to form by putting together
	construct	to arrange parts or elements; to build
	convince	to persuade by argument; establish belief
	create	to produce or bring about by a course of action
	deduce	to derive from
	design	to conceive and plan
	develop	to expound; to make clear by degrees or in detail
	devise	to plan to obtain or bring about
	effect	to bring about, or cause to take place
	eliminate	to exclude based on specified criteria
	enact	to set up, establish, or constitute
	enlist	to secure the support and aid of; employ
	equalize	to make like in quality or quantity
	erect	to put together by the fitting of materials; build
	establish	to set up or constitute
	excite	to stimulate to action
	exhibit	to present to view
	finish	to complete
	formulate	to form in a systematized manner
	give	to furnish what is needed
	inaugurate	to bring about the beginning

Skill	Verb	Definition
Problem Solving (Continued)	incite	to move to action
	include	to incorporate based on specified criteria
	initiate	to cause the beginning of; set in motion
	introduce	to bring into play; institute
	invent	to originate, find, begin
	launch	to set in motion; initiate
	make	to create or cause to exist, occur, or appear
	originate	to author or cause to exist
	plot	to devise or plan to bring about
	present	to offer to view; show
	produce	to make, yield, render, or bring to bear
	show	to cause or permit to be seen; exhibit
	stimulate	to arouse to action
	supply	to furnish what is needed; give
Cognitive Strategy	accede to	to give in to a request or demand
	accept	to regard as having a certain meaning; understand
	admit	to allow or permit; provide for
	advocate	to plead in favor of
	affirm	to validate
	agree to	to settle on by common consent; admit; concede
	allow	to permit, admit, consent say or state
	approve	to give formal or official sanction
	arrange	to place or distribute in an orderly manner
	authorize	to establish by authority
	champion	to uphold; support
	clarify	to make understandable
	comply	to accept tacitly or overtly
	concede to	to accept as true, valid or accurate
	confirm	to give approval to; ratify
	contain	to have within; hold; compromise; include
	corroborate	to support with evidence or authority; confirm
	defend	to protect or defend a position

Skill	Verb	Definition
Cognitive Strategy (Continued)	define	to fix or mark limits
	describe	to represent or give an account
	embrace	to include
	employ	to make use of
	enact	to establish by legal and authoritative action
	encompass	to enclose, envelop, or include
	endorse	to express approval publicly
	endure	to remain firm or unyielding
	engage	to attract and hold
	espouse	to give verbal support
	exercise	to make effective; use; exert
	exhaust	to use up or consume entirely
	expend	to make use for a specific purpose
	explain	to make known; to make plain and understandable
	implement	to put into effect, carry out, or accomplish
	incorporate	to unite or work into something that already exists so as to form an indistinguishable whole
	incur	to contract
	legislate	to enact by laws
	list	to enumerate
	manipulate	to manage or use skillfully
	narrate	to tell in detail
	operate	to perform a function; to produce an appropriate effect
	permit	to make possible
	prove	to test the truth or validity of
	ratify	to formally approve and sanction; confirm
	recite	to repeat or read aloud
	recount	to relate in detail; narrate
	rehearse	to present an account of; repeat, narrate; relate or enumerate
	relate	to give an account of; tell
	report	to give an account of
	sanction	to make valid or binding

Skill	Verb	Definition
Cognitive Strategy (Continued)	simplify	to make more intelligible
	substantiate	to establish by proof or evidence; verify
	support	to substantiate
	uphold	to support against an opponent
	use	to put into action
	validate	to confirm, support, or corroborate
	verify	to confirm or substantiate in law by oath
Verbal Information	acknowledge	to make known or take notice
	advance	to move forward
	affirm	to state positively; validate or confirm
	agree	to be consistent or in harmony with
	allege	to assert without proof
	announce	to make known publicly; proclaim
	argue	to contend or disagree in words; dispute
	articulate	to express
	assert	to state or declare positively
	attest	to establish or verify the usage of
	characterize	to describe the character or quality
	charge	to command or instruct
	clarify	to make understandable
	comment	to explain or interpret
	communicate	to make known
	confess	to tell or make known
	confirm	to approve or ratify
	contend	to maintain or assert
	contribute	to supply information
	decipher	to convert into intelligible form
	declare	to make known formally or explicitly
	decode	to decipher
	define	to explain the meaning of
	delineate	to describe in detail
	describe	to represent or give an account of
	explain	to make known; to make understandable

Skill	Verb	Definition
Verbal Information (Continued)	expound	to set forth; state
	express	to represent, state, depict, or delineate
	interpret	to explain or tell the meaning of
	justify	to prove or show to be just, right, or reasonable
	narrate	to tell in detail
	notify	to give notice
	offer	to present for acceptance
	portray	to describe in words
	profess	to declare or admit openly or freely
	propose	to set forth
	rationalize	to bring into accord with reason or cause something to seem reasonable
	recount	to relate in detail or narrate
	speak	to talk
	tell	to state or relate
	utter	to speak
	summarize	to describe briefly and succinctly
	verbalize	to express in words
	vocalize	to speak
	voice	to express in words
Motor Skill	attach	to fasten to
	administer	to manager or supervise the use of
	aid	to help
	arrange	to order
	bring about	to cause to take place
	bring on	to cause to appear
	carry out	to achieve
	clean	to remove or eradicate; strip or empty
	complete	to finish
	conduct	to lead
	deal	to distribute
	deliver	to convey

Skill	Verb	Definition
Motor Skill	demonstrate	to show
(Continued)	direct	to show or point out
	discharge	to unload
	dismiss	to permit or cause to leave
	dispense	to deal out in portions
	display	to make evident
	distribute	to expend by proportion
	do	to bring to pass or carry out
	donate	to give
	dramatize	to present with heightened action
	emerge	to come forth
	empty	to remove the contents of
	endow	to bestow upon or furnish with
	equip	to furnish
	establish	to physically erect
	excrete	to sift out; discharge
	finish	to bring to an end
	force	to cause to happen
	free	to rid of restraints
	give	to yield, grant, or bestow
	impersonate	to assume the character of or act like another
	implement	to carry out; accomplish
	inflict	to impose or perpetrate
	liberate	to set free
	make	to create or construct
	organize	to arrange
	pass	to move ahead of
	perform	to act out or dramatize
	play	to engage in pleasurable activity
	present	to show
	release	to let go
	serve	to wait upon
	sketch	to draw
	stage	to produce for public view

Skill	Verb	Definition
Motor Skill (Continued)	supply	to provide for
	surrender	to give over
	transfer	to convey from one person, place, or situation to another
	work	to expend energy toward labor
Attitude	adopt	to accept formally
	advocate	to plead in favor of
	champion	to support
	complete	to finish
	conclude	to decide
	cull	to select from a group
	decide	to come to a conclusion
	decree	to determine
	defend	to take a position
	determine	to settle or decide
	discover	to make known or visible
	discriminate	to distinguish
	distinguish	to perceive a difference
	divine	to discover or locate
	elect	to choose freely
	embrace	to take in or include as part of
	encompass	to include
	endorse	to express approval
	espouse	to support
	fancy	to like
	favor	to lean toward
	include	to take in as part of a whole
	incorporate	to unite or work into something that already exists
	judge	to form an opinion of
	opt	to choose or select
	perform	to act out or dramatize
	pick	to choose or select
	prefer	to like better; recommend

Skill	Verb	Definition
Attitude	resolve	to conclude
(Continued)	select	to choose by preference
	settle	to resolve or decide
	state	to say
	take up	to accept or adopt

APPENDIX B

AUTHORING SYSTEMS

Authoring Systems

The following list of CBT Authoring Systems is reprinted from the November, 1993 issue of *CBT Solutions*, which was, in turn, reprinted from SB Communications' *1993 Computer Based Training Report.* The complete citation is found in the References section for Unit 4, Development.

Authoring Systems Most Often Identified by Respondents	
Authoring Product	No. of Mentions
Authorware	56
ToolBook	52
Quest	38
IconAuthor	31
TenCore	30
Phoenix	22
HyperCard	19
ACT III	15
TIE	15
LinkWay	14
Authology	10
Sage	10
SAM	10
Director	9
Demo II	7
PC Pilot	7
Summit	7
MicroTICCIT	6

NOTE: We do not endorse any of these authoring systems but remind you that the needs of the customer are paramount in the choice of authoring systems.

APPENDIX C

LIST OF ACRONYMS AND ABBREVIATIONS

List of Acronyms and Abbreviations

ANOVA	Analysis of Variance
BBS	Bulletin Board Services
CAI	Computer Assisted Instruction
CBT	Computer Based Training
CC	Configuration Control
CD ROM	Compact Disk Read Only Memory
CDS	Course Design Specifications
CRT	Criterion-Referenced Test
CU	Close Up
DVI	Digital Video Interactive
ECU	Extreme Close Up
EEOC	Equal Employment Opportunity Commission
ELS	Extreme Long Shot
EO	Enabling Objective
EPIE	Educational Products Information Exchange
ERIC	Educational Resources Information Center
ID	Instructional Designer
ID&D	Instructional Design & Development
ISD	Instructional Systems Design
IVD	Interactive Videodisc
KSA	Knowledge, Skills, and Attitudes
LS	Long Shot
LO	Lesson Objective
MIS	Management Information Systems
MS	Medium Shot
NRT	Norm-Referenced Test
RAO	Rank And Order
RFP	Request For Proposal
ROI	Return On Investment
SAT	Scholastic Aptitude Test
SB	Storyboard
SME	Subject Matter Expert
SPSS	Statistical Package for the Social Sciences
TO	Terminal Objective
VATK	Visual, Auditory, Tactile, Kinesthetic

APPENDIX D

STATISTICAL MEASUREMENT TESTS

Statistical Measurement Tests

Correlations

Biserial Correlation

Biserial correlation is a test that can be used when one variable is a continuous score and the other is a dichotomy. For example, if you want to predict the success of a manager in his or her position based on the score on a test of management capability skills, you could use this test. The score on the management test is the continuous variable and the success of the manager is the dichotomy. The dichotomy is not a pure dichotomy because there are varying degrees of success among managers. This measure can be used for norm- or criterion-referenced analysis.

Kendall's tau

Kendall's tau is used the same way that the rank difference correlations are used but with extremely small numbers of cases ($n < 10$). This is a norm-referenced measurement.

Kuder Richardson Test of Split Half Reliability (KR-20)

Split half reliability is another measure used to determine if two test versions are equal. It involves splitting the test into two tests (i.e., by putting all even numbered questions on one test, and all odd numbered questions on another) and administering the two tests to the same groups that just completed the training course. The subsequent correlation will indicate whether the two tests are of the same level of difficulty. Therefore, the overall test does not have any unusually difficult questions.

Pearson Product Moment Correlation (Pearson r)

Product Moment Correlation is a norm-referenced testing measure to use when you want to compare how a score on one test compares with the score on another test, both of which have two continuous variables. For example, you can compare a test that you developed with a test that has already been standardized.

Phi Coefficient (Φ)

This is a test to correlate two variables that are both true dichotomies. For example, you can determine the correlation between two test items on a test as they were answered by one student. This can be used as a criterion-referenced measure.

An example of a place to use this test is when you have a lengthy test where there are two questions that are based on the same objective, but each question is asked in a different way. Your purpose might be to determine if students answer one question correctly and the other incorrectly. Your data will give you the answer to the question but you then need to examine further to determine if it is because the students did not know the answer and got the one simply by guessing, or if they got one wrong because it was improperly worded.

Point-biserial Correlation

Point-biserial correlation is a test that can be used when one variable is a continuous score and the other is a true dichotomy. For example, you may want to determine how the response on one particular test question by a group of students compares with their overall score on a test. Your continuous variable is the scores on the overall test; your dichotomy is if the student got the test item correct — Yes or No. Point-biserial correlation is a criterion-referenced measure.

Rank Difference Correlation

Rank difference correlations are used the same way as product moment correlation but are used when the number of cases is less than 30 (n < 30). Again, this a norm-referenced measure — not to be used in CRT.

Tests of Significance

Analysis of Variance (ANOVA)

Analysis of Variance is used to compare more than two means. Suppose you want to compare the groups described in the t-Test above on more than two characteristics. For example, you might want to compare the scores on a performance test using the variables of sex, ethnic background, and previous training, The ANOVA will compare all of these variables and let you know which are significant in relation to the others.

Chi-square Test

The Chi-square test is used to compare two sets of frequency data — one that is dichotomous and one that is continuous. For example, you may want to compare whether a student was able to perform a task on a series of attempts. The continuous score would be the number of attempts allowed, and the dichotomy would be "correct" or "incorrect." The Chi-square test is a non-parametric measure well suited to most CRTs. Non-parametric tests do not assume a normal distribution of the scores.

Mann Whitney Test

The Mann Whitney test allows you to compare groups of unequal size on a particular variable. For example, if a study that was conducted by a researcher in the past using a population of 1000 subjects produced certain results, you can compare a study that you have conducted using only 50 subjects to determine if both came to the same conclusion on that particular variable.

t-Test of Significance

A t-Test compares the significance between the means of two samples to determine if one is significantly different from the other. For example, you may want to compare the scores of a sub-group of a population based on one characteristic and compare that to the scores of the entire population. Your results determine whether the scores of the two groups are independent (have no connection) or are dependent (interrelated — have a connection). You can use a **one-tailed** test to determine the difference at one of the two ends of the distribution curve or a **two-tailed** test to determine significance at both ends of the distribution curve.

GLOSSARY

Application Software A specific tool to which a computer program or software package is dedicated.

Assessment/Analysis The terminology in this book given to the first phase of the ISD Process to better show the two distinct parts of the phase (i.e., Assessment and Front-end Analysis).

Authoring Facility A generic term to refer to both authoring systems and authoring languages.

Authoring Languages Software packages that require programming to demonstrate the capabilities of the language but which are capable of producing very sophisticated training products.

Authoring Systems Software packages that allow for very sophisticated development with a minimum of programming required. These may include icon-based systems and systems so sophisticated that they can take information input through fill-in-the-blank prompts and format it as questions, text, etc., with a system of pre-structured templates. They can also be object-based where you enter exactly what you want in the program. What you see is what you get.

Branching Part of programming logic that moves (jumps) to another part of the program because of an input from a student.

Check Disk (or Disc) The first disk that is returned from the technical production house that is used to check that all material is on the disk and of the level of quality required.

Computer Based Training (CBT) Training that uses the interactive delivery medium of a computer, either in part or entirely.

Concurrent Validity Measures of the ability of test items to discriminate between master and novice students by having representatives of both groups take the test. Establishes the superiority of a course in instructional delivery when the course will be used for certification of competence.

Configuration In computer systems, a specific combination of equipment. Also known as a platform.

Congruence	The match that occurs between the objective, the course content, and the test item within a lesson that ensures that the material is presented and tested at the appropriate taxonomic level.
Content Validity	Measures that employ experts to review materials and qualitatively validate that there is congruence between the objectives, content, and test items.
Correlation	Establishes the relationship between two variables regarding whether one variable is dependent upon the other for the dependent variable to be true. The result is a number between −1.0 and +1.0. The closer the correlation to +1.0, the higher the positive correlation and the stronger the correlation.
Course Design Specifications (CDS)	The document that contains the standards by which a course will be produced.
Criterion-Referenced Test (CRT)	Measures of performance against a predetermined standard that allows the comparison of individual students against that standard.
Cueing	Providing hints in the form of additional information that will help a student answer a question correctly after an incorrect answer is given.
Debug	The process of reviewing CBT to remove all branching or other functional errors from the programming.
Dichotomy	The division of a class of people or objects into two distinctly different groups.
Difficulty Index	A rating score by subject matter experts that identifies how high a degree of expertise would be necessary for a student to correctly answer a particular test item.
Digital Video Interactive (DVI)	A technology from Intel that supports various levels of quality for still and moving images encoded and decoded from hard disks and optical disks.
Distractor Analysis	Analysis of the possible answers (distractors) on a test to determine if there are certain questions that students are consistently answering incorrectly, and if a certain one of the incorrect distractors is being chosen more prevalently than any of the others.

Exemplary Performers	Those job holders who exhibit superior skills and abilities in the KSA to be trained. In performance training, you don't want to train to the average performer; what is needed is the most efficient performance to produce the highest quality results. These are the same persons who should be your SMEs from the customer's facility.
Face Validity	Qualitative measures that require SME validation that course content approximates that of any other course on the subject. It is the minimum validity required to establish that a course teaches what it intends to teach or test. It cannot be the only form of validity used if reliability measures are also required.
Format (n)	The physical or technical specifications of data that define specific hardware and software products and encoding techniques.
Format (v)	To prepare data or media according to specific technical criteria.
Formative Evaluation	Within the CBT context, all activities that occur from the time a customer begins contract negotiations until the final product is delivered that ensure the instructional soundness, quality, and suitability of a training program.
Functional Review	A review of CBT courseware to determine if the programming (i.e., branching, forward/backward movement) operates correctly.
General Purpose Languages	Computer languages that were not originally designed to support training development.
Glass Master	A glass model original of a laser disc onto which all audio and video is inscribed with a laser beam. This "master disc" is used to make copies of the final plastic videodisc through the use of a stamper that impresses the exact image from the master disc onto the plastic.
Hard Card	The permanent hard disk inside the computer, as opposed to a floppy disk inserted in a disk drive.
High End Authoring Languages/Systems	Software packages that permit the integration of many different sources of multimedia, highly sophisticated and high resolution visual displays, and extensive capabilities for inputs and responses. These require many enhancements over the computer usually found in the office, such as increased RAM, hard disk storage, and many peripherals.

Hotspots	Areas of the computer screen that, when chosen (touched with a cursor or some input device), initiate specific actions or responses.
Icon	A graphics window associated with a certain, pre-encoded, function in an authoring system or language.
Input	A point in a computer program that requires the student to insert information by responding with information that was derived from a thought process. Simply pressing a key to continue to another screen is not considered an input, within the CBT context.
Input Devices	Keyboards, light pens, touch screens, trackballs, joysticks, or any other device that allows students to respond to the computer in some manner.
Instructional Development and Design (ID&D)	One of the numerous names for the five phases involved in the production of training or instructional materials. Synonym for Instructional Systems Design (ISD).
Instructional Systems Design (ISD)	One of the numerous names for the five phases involved in the production of training or instructional materials. Usually referred to as the system developed by Robert Gagné and Leslie Briggs. The five phases are Analysis, Design, Development, Implementation, and Evaluation. Synonym for Instructional Design and Development (ID&D).
Instrument Validity	Developing and evaluating test instruments to ensure the informational data collected is unbiased and able to be replicated during subsequent administrations of the instrument.
Interactive Video	Information systems that combine sound and pictures form a videodisc with the text, graphics, and processing done via a micro-processor; generally through a delivery system that includes a monitor and input devices.
Item Analysis	A test that compares two independent variables to determine if individual test items are valid. Item analysis will require different statistical tests to be applied, depending on the information required.

Leptokurtic Curve	A positively or negatively skewed distribution curve where the mean near the top or bottom end of the distribution with unequal standard deviations above or below the mean. Also known as a Mastery Curve.
Linear	A computer program that provides little or no branching based on individual student inputs but, rather, moves through a program much as a page of a book turns.
Low End Authoring Languages/Systems	Software packages that permit limited amounts and types of multimedia (usually only graphics and animation) but have the advantage of being able to be run from nearly any computer by inserting a floppy disk and running the course directly from the disk or loading the courseware on the hard disk and running it from there. Certain hardware and software capabilities are required for varying authoring systems (certain amounts of RAM, internal memory, monitor display capabilities), but most requirements are found on the average office computers; there is no need for extended internal components or other hardware peripherals.
Management Review	A review of courseware by the internal management for the purpose of determining if the product meets contractual requirements.
Master Disc	A glass model original of a laser disc onto which all audio and video is inscribed with a laser beam. This "glass master" is used to make copies of the final plastic videodisc through the use of a stamper that impresses the exact image from the master disc onto the plastic.
Mastering	The process of converting data from a master tape to a master disc.
Mastery Curve	A distribution curve with a mean near the upper or lower end of the distribution indicating that the majority of the group whose characteristic is shown on the curve has or does not have the attribute. Also known as a Leptokurtic Curve.
Mastery Learning	Overlearning a concept or skill to the point where it can be performed automatically (without conscious attention paid to each component of the concept or skill).

Metacognition	The approach to learning that does not deal with teaching content but rather presents strategies to students that teach students "how to learn." For example, rather than teaching reading comprehension (remembering what one reads) by asking questions about what was read, metacognitive strategies teach "ways of remembering" what was read. Or rather than improving memory by having students memorize lists, teaches ways to organize lists into common elements or the use of mnemonic devices (like the first letter of each phrase makes a sentence or word) to remember things.
Modality	Referring to the senses of vision, hearing, and touch; the method that a person uses to learn. The preferred learning sensory mode. Often associated with the VATK (Visual, Auditory, Tactile, Kinesthetic) system of learning.
Motivation	The basic desire to move toward a goal or objective. External motivation is that which creates the desire through a force outside of the individual (i.e., external rewards such as money, love, food). Internal motivation is that which comes from within the individual (i.e., the personal satisfaction of accomplishment or success).
Multimedia (in CBT)	The integration of various sources (such as audio, video, text, graphics) into one system that delivers information, under computer control.
Normal Curve	A distribution curve that graphically shows the results from a group where each is compared on the same variable; the average (mean) score is near the middle of the distribution with equal intervals (standard deviations) both above and below the mean.
Normal Distribution	A distribution where the mean is near the middle of the distribution with equal intervals (standard deviations) both above and below the mean.
Norm-Referenced Test (NRT)	Measures of knowledge or performance against a level that is derived from the averages of all scores from a large sample of students' performance on the test. This measure allows comparisons of those who should possess the same characteristic.
Overlearning	Learning to the mastery level where skills and knowledge become truly integrated into the knowledge or skill base of the student; learning to the automatic level.

Platform	Any configuration of computer hardware used to develop and/or deliver CBT.
Predictive Validity	Measures of the ability of a test to predict future success in a skill area as a result of success on a test. Establishes superiority of a course in instructional delivery when the course will be used for certification of competence.
Production Baseline Storyboards	Finalized storyboards after the Pre-production meeting from which the actual CBT lesson is produced.
Qualitative	Subjective measures of instructional soundness. May be open to a variety of interpretations.
Quantitative	Measures of instructional soundness that employ data and the results of statistical analyses.
Reinforcement	An internal or external stimulus that causes a student to want to continue or repeat (positive reinforcement) or not repeat (negative reinforcement) an action.
Reliability	A quantifiable value that describes the degree to which a training program produces consistent results in what it teaches.
Screen	One event or concept depicted on the computer monitor separated by the <Enter> input required by the student.
Simulations	CBT-generated scenarios that contain a high degree of realism regarding the actual situation as it would actually be experienced. High level simulations duplicate complex situations where the student actually experiences and reacts to the scenario; mid and low level simulations demonstrate a situation but have students input answers to questions after the scenario.
Skewed Distribution	A distribution on a curve where the mean is clustered around the top or bottom end of the curve with unequal intervals (standard deviations) on either side of the mean.
Standardized	Repeated administrations of a test to refine the test to the point where it is both valid and reliable (students will score consistently on the test) resulting in a normal distribution curve from any group of people who possess or should possess a certain characteristic.

Standards Review	A review of courseware according to the requirements set forth in the Course Design Specifications.
Subject Matter Expert (SME)	A person with a high degree of expertise on the skill or concept who can be used to provide consultation on technical content aspects of design and development of a CBT project.
Summative Evaluation	Testing the effectiveness of the training program along predetermined criteria.
Technical Review	A review to ensure the technical content accuracy of training.
Test Item Validity	Statistical analysis of test items to ensure they measure the skills learned to a sufficiently high degree to discriminate between high-achieving and low-achieving students.
Time-out	A screen with a timer set so that the program will move to the next screen after a certain amount of time.
Validation	Procedures employed to ensure the instructional effectiveness of a training program.
Validity	A quantifiable value that describes the degree to which a training program teaches what it claims to teach.

Index

6526

ABOUT THE AUTHORS

The authors and contributors bring to this book seventy-five years of experience in the field of education and training. They have successfully created training courses for all delivery media (instructor, self-paced, videotape, audiotape).

Dr. William W. Lee earned his Ph.D. from Penn State University in 1986 in Curriculum Development and Instruction. His Master's of Education is also from Penn State and his Bachelor's of Education was earned at Clarion University of Pennsylvania. He has taught at three universities and worked in business and industry since 1987. His thesis at Penn State established the first software evaluation instrument to assess the critical components of computer software for use with learning disabled individuals. He is widely published and regularly presents at regional, national, and international conferences. He holds several copyrights on software evaluation instruments, evaluation hierarchies, an instructional design process, and an organizational development process. He has worked and/or consulted for numerous major corporations in the United States and overseas.

Robert A. Mamone earned his M.Ed. in Instructional Design and Technology at the University of Pittsburgh where he is now a doctoral candidate in the same program. He holds a B.A. from St. Peter's College, Jersey City, New Jersey and has completed Laurea Studies at the Universita' degli Studi in Rome, Italy. He has designed and developed training for all types of delivery media in the United States as well as the Middle East and Southeast Asia. These training courses are in use at all organizational levels and in national training programs. He has developed training for the manufacturing and service industries, working in both the private and public sectors. He holds a copyright on a software evaluation hierarchy.

Kenneth A. Roadman contributes thirty years of experience in instructional design and program management to this book. He received his Ed.D. in Instructional Design Technology from Penn State in 1986 and has since worked for national and multi-national companies on projects ranging from weapon systems to aircraft simulators.